50 Places in Rome, Florence, and Venice Every Woman Should Go

SUSAN VAN ALLEN

TRAVELERS' TALES
AN IMPRINT OF SOLAS HOUSE, INC.
PALO ALTO

Travelers' Tales and Solas House are trademarks of Solas House, Inc.,
2320 Bowdoin Street, Palo Alto, California 94306. www.travelerstales.com

Art Direction: Stefan Gutermuth
Cover Photograph: @ leoks (Shutterstock)
Author Photograph: Veronica Puleo, VeroFoto
Interior Design and Page Layout: Howie Severson

Distributed by Publishers Group West, 1700 Fourth Street, Berkeley, CA 94170

Library of Congress Cataloging-in-Publication Data
Van Allen, Susan.
  50 places in Rome, Florence and Venice every woman should go / Susan Van
Allen. -- First edition.
       pages cm -- (100 places)
  Summary: "With passion, humor, and helpful details, this book inspires readers to discover masterpieces, sensual delights, and adventures in Italy's best cities. Susan Van Allen, savvy girlfriend whispering in readers' ears, cuts through
guidebook gobbledygook and steers women to create the Italian vacation of their
dreams"-- Provided by publisher.
  ISBN 978-1-60952-096-0 (paperback) -- ISBN 1-60952-096-3 (paperback)
  1. Rome (Italy)--Guidebooks. 2. Florence (Italy)--Guidebooks. 3. Venice
(Italy)--Guidebooks. 4. Women--Travel--Italy--Guidebooks. 5. Women travel-
ers--Italy--Guidebooks. 6. Italy--Guidebooks. I. Title. II. Title: Fifty places in
Rome, Florence and Venice every woman should go.
  DG804.V24 2014
  914.56'3204--dc23
                                    2014032561

First Edition
Printed in the United States
10 9 8 7 6 5 4 3 2 1

"Susan Van Allen's writing makes the magic of Italy jump off the page. She has a knack for capturing the charms, quirks and authenticity of this magnificent land. Don't go to Italy without reading this!"

—Kathy McCabe, Editor and Publisher,
Dream of Italy Travel Newsletter

"Italy has a new portrait: sexy and savvy. 100 Places makes a gal smile in English and Italian, to eat up this compendium of Italy's most delectable women's outings."

—Anne Calcagno, author of *Pray For Yourself*

"No matter how many times you've been to Italy and think you know it, reading Susan Van Allen's book almost guarantees a return trip...a delightful book you'll only put down long enough to check the flights to that fascinating country."

—Carol Coviello-Malzone, author of
Flavors of Rome: How, What & Where to Eat in the Eternal City

"Susan Van Allen is taking the travel book industry by storm... The practical information combined with intriguing details are a must have for those who are hunting for the hidden gems d'Italia."

—*Bell'Avventura*

Males Weigh In:

"Part guidebook, part history, and part manual to the good life in the land of La Dolce Vita, Susan Van Allen's magnum opus on all things Italian is essential reading for women (and men) who either want to get the most out of their next trip or want to be spirited back to their last."

—David Farley, author of *An Irreverent Curiosity*

"That old Freudian chestnut—'What do women really want?!' has been answered once again. Susan Van Allen has romped through Italy and picked the very best, mixing dreamy delights with drops of dainty decadence. She suggests readers: "treat this book like a cookbook...and make a full meal of it." ...you could—and you should."

—David Yeadon, author of *Seasons in Basilicata*

To my grandparents, Nana and Papa,
who sent postcards from Italy

Italy is a dream that keeps returning for the rest of your life.

—ANNA AKHMATOVA, RUSSIAN POET

Table of Contents

Preface:
Italy's Big Three

ROME, FLORENCE, VENICE...Say the words and iconic images emerge: Colosseum, Duomo, Grand Canal.

These places first dazzled me in postcards, sent by Papa, my grandfather, who traveled back to Italy, his homeland, every August. They'd clunk into the metal mailbox of the ranch house I grew up in on the Jersey shore. I'd stare into those postcards of fountains and piazzas, glancing up at our flat backyard of scruffy grass and a rusty jungle gym, Country Squire Station Wagon in the driveway. Could this be real?

Travel dreams came true, and I stepped off trains into the abundant pleasures of Italy, beyond postcards, to the taste of my first Roman artichoke, smells of leather shops in Florence, songs of gondoliers.

Decades of travel and making lists of advice for girlfriends inspired my first book, *100 Places in Italy Every Woman Should Go*. Wonderful surprises followed—letters, meetings with readers from far-flung places, who came back with thanks and stories of their Italian adventures.

Men tell me: "It's not just for women!" I agree, though the fact is this: Something clicks with us females, from the moment we touch down in Italy, and we're surrounded by goddesses and Madonnas. We immediately feel lightened up, unbound, welcomed by the spirit of the pleasure-loving goddess Venus and the compassionate Blessed Virgin Mother, who side by side inspire us to enjoy every step we take.

This book is an invitation to discover the Big Three beyond the postcards and to revel in their feminine appeals—from such delights as paintings in Florence where females are glorified, churches in Rome that honor female saints, and places where women have flourished, such as Peggy Guggenheim's museum in Venice. I guide you to have fun in my favorite caffès, gelaterias, shop in the best places for ceramics or jewelry, and treat yourself to adventures—be it rowing in Venice, jewelry making in Florence, or a cooking school in Rome.

With so many treasures to choose from, Italy may be overwhelming, so I urge you to follow your mood and open yourself to spontaneity. Rather than Must See lists, I propose Golden Days—matching one site with a nearby great restaurant, not packing too much in, but savoring your time Italian style, at an Old World pace.

May you find yourself inside those postcard images, experiencing The Real Rome, Florence, and Venice—blending in with all their beauties that welcome you with open arms.

Buon Viaggio!
SUSAN VAN ALLEN, HOLLYWOOD

I

Rome

"I came to Rome at the age of 50 to see how beautiful ruins can be."
—IRIS CARULLI, ROME TOUR GUIDE

Rome begins with Venus, Goddess of Love and Beauty. Ancient Romans believed they were her descendants. It was Venus who seduced a Greek mortal and thus became the great grandmother of Romulus and Remus, those twins suckled by a she-wolf on Rome's Palatine Hill who founded the Eternal City.

Her presence is eternal. If you have doubts, watch Roman women striding down the Via del Corso, knowing that spark of Venus lives within them.

The bold, vibrant city has always attracted pleasure seekers—from the days of Empresses to *Roman Holiday* times when Audrey Hepburn spun around the ruins on a Vespa. Blending with the pleasures is the Madonna—dangling off taxicab mirrors, popping out of alleyway altars, wowing you in masterpieces. Her motherly love mixes with the sensual spirit of Venus, beckoning you to let go and enjoy. After all, *Roma* is *Amor*, Love spelled backwards, so open your heart to all she offers.

It's a city that brings pleasures for lifetimes, so be sure to toss your coin in the Fountain of Trevi to ensure you'll return.

Along with my suggestions, other major attractions:

Vatican Museums-Sistine Chapel: The climax of your visit here is Michelangelo's masterpiece ceiling (with glorious sibyls—female prophets) and the Raphael rooms, but along the way be sure to detour to the Pinacoteca to see the tapestries by Raphael and beautiful Madonnas by Renaissance masters. (mv.vatican.va)

Colosseum: Where noblewomen came in the days of the empire and the great novelty of women gladiator shows took place. (www.coopculture.it)

TIP: *Be sure to buy tickets in advance for the Vatican Museums and Colosseum to avoid long lines. Better yet, check out the Online Resources and join a guided tour.*

RECOMMENDED READING

Travelers' Tales Italy edited by Anne Calcagno

30 Days in Italy edited by James O'Reilly, Larry Habegger, and Sean O'Reilly

1 The Campidoglio, Roman Forum, and Palatine Hill

YOU'LL NEVER FORGET YOUR FIRST TIME. You'll be walking along or speeding in a cab from the airport and then will appear... the Colosseum...the Arco di Tito...the whole glorious spread of jaw-dropping triumph and ruin.

It's a place to let your imagination run wild. Picture women rattling tambourines in torch-lit processions, chariots carrying tanned muscular men in togas to the baths.

Goddesses' temples, Empresses' tombs, and churches dedicated to the Virgin Mary are all to be discovered in the thousand-plus years of history that surround you. It's impossible to absorb it all in one shot. Hiring a good guide is best since hardly any of the sculptures and ruins are marked. Or just stroll around and surrender to your fantasies.

Here are some places where women take center stage:

The Campidoglio

The Michelangelo-designed piazza is a perfect place to begin, where **Minerva, Goddess of Wisdom, Rome, and War,** sits on a throne holding her mighty spear—just behind Marcus Aurelius on his horse. To either side of Minerva are the Capitoline

Museums, packed with sculptures of characters who once roamed the area surrounding you.

In the **Palazzo Nuovo** (museum to the left of Minerva) head to the first-floor hallway to see *The Capitoline Venus*. The Goddess of Love and Beauty is featured in a sunlit niche, posed as Venus *Pudica* (modest Venus), with one hand over her breast, the other covering her Cupid's cloister. Yes, she's modest, but also teasing, as if to say: "Look what I'm hiding..."

Venus was the deity who flitted from passion to passion. She was married to Vulcan, God of Fire, but even the best couple's counselor couldn't have kept this beauty tied to that angry, crippled god. Venus had hot affairs with Mars (God of War), the devastatingly handsome Adonis, and disguised herself as a mortal for trysts with men she found attractive. Every year she bathed herself in the sea from which she was born to renew her virginity.

In the same hallway, you'll see a statue of a **Roman Woman Dressed as Venus** (hardly dressed), proving how closely Romans associated themselves with the goddess. The Roman woman breaks out of the Modest Venus pose, standing proud and naked with one hand on her hip. For a laugh farther down the hall, check out the **Drunken Old Woman**, who's crouched, laughing, and guzzling a jug of wine.

Santa Maria d'Aracoeli
(Saint Mary of the Altar of Heaven)

Up steep steps from the Palazzo Nuovo is this red brick church, dedicated to Mary. It was built over a temple that was dedicated to Juno (Goddess of Marriage). The legend goes that in ancient times a sibyl (wise woman prophet) appeared here to Emperor Augustus and foretold the coming of Christ. The stairs were called *The Stairway to Heaven* in Medieval times, when women want-ing a child or husband would climb them on their knees.

The Roman Forum

Here in the ongoing archaeological excavation, you'll see ancient Rome's largest temple, dedicated to **Venus and Rome**. It was built during Emperor Hadrian's time, now distinguished by its large curved half roof. Once it held two humongous stat-ues of those beloved deities, sitting on thrones, back to back. Roman priests would sacrifice female animals to these goddesses to bring good fortune in war and business.

Nearby is the **Temple of the Vestal Virgins**, now rows of pillars with remains of female statues.

The Cult of **Vesta, Goddess of Hearth and Home**, was the oldest of the ancient world. Some say this cult still exists in modern Italy, where *la famiglia* remains the country's core. Back then, girls from the ages of six to ten were chosen from patrician families to become Vestals, taking vows of chastity and service for thirty years. They tended the temple flames, made salt cakes, and were the only women presiding at rituals.

The upside for the Vestals, in a time when women didn't have that much freedom, was that they could come and go as they pleased and got perks all over town, like special seats at games and festivals. The downside was gruesome: if they let Vesta's flame go out, they'd be flogged, and if they had sex with anyone, they'd be buried alive.

The Palatine Hill

Walking up from the Forum, you come to this pretty and serene place, where Romulus (great grandson of Venus) chose to begin

the city. It went on to become the Beverly Hills of Ancient
Rome, where noble palaces were built. In the sixteenth century
the Farnese family created gardens here, so you can wander
through rows of boxwood shrubs, cypress trees, laurel and rose
bushes, and enjoy lovely views of the Forum below.

As for the palaces, the **Home of Augustus** is now open to the
public, but be prepared to wait in a long line to see the emper-
or's frescos unless you get there when the site opens. His wife
Livia's house is going through restoration, and you may be
lucky to find it open and then be treated to a vast arched space
with frescos of vibrant garlands, symbols of Augustus's victories.
The Palatine is a great place to fantasize about the grand days of
Livia and Augustus, who ruled Rome for forty-five years, bringing the city into its Golden Age.

Back in 39 B.C., just after Julius Caesar's
assassination, Livia was a beautiful nineteen-
year-old, married to the much older Tiberius
Claudius Nero and pregnant with their second child. Along came handsome, young,
Octavius (soon to be Augustus), a rising star
on the military scene, married with a pregnant
wife. Octavius fell in love with Livia, divorced his wife the day
she gave birth, and married the pregnant Livia. Livia's old husband gave her away at the ceremony, even throwing in a dowry.
It turned out to be a good political move for all involved, and in
those days the citizenry didn't even blink over it.

Octavius became Emperor Caesar Augustus and ruled Rome
with his perfect mate Livia, who took charge of all the biz at
home when he set off to conquer distant lands. Livia was an
exemplary Roman wife. She was famously chaste, "worked wool"

(made her husband's togas), and never showed off with fancy jewelry or dress. The couple lived simply here throughout their fifty-one years of marriage, with Livia putting up with philandering Augustus, who was known for his S&M exploits. Together they revived Rome, restoring monuments in the Forum and building new ones throughout the city.

Livia has become famous in fiction, particularly through Robert Graves's *I Claudius*, where she's portrayed as a conniving woman who poisoned potential heirs to make sure her family line would inherit the throne. Whatever version of the story you believe, Livia's descendants did end up ruling Rome. She died at the ripe old age of eighty-six and was honored as Diva Augusta. Her image was revered in the streets that surround you, carried in celebrations by elephant-drawn carriages.

To get a more vivid experience of Livia's lifestyle, head to the **Palazzo Massimo alle Terme**, near Roma Termini. The entire garden room of her suburban villa has been moved to the top floor of this museum, so you can stand in the midst of amazing frescos that feature a harmonious, abundant landscape of trees, flowers, and birds.

Capitoline Museums: Tuesday through Sunday, 9–8 (www.turismoroma.it)

Roman Forum and Palatine Hill: Daily, 8:30 until one hour before sunset. For opening times of House of Augustus and Livia's House (www.coopculture.it)

Palazzo Massimo alle Terme: Largo di Villa Peretti 1 (near Termini), Tuesday–Sunday 9–7:30 (www.archeoromabeniculturali.it)

❧

Golden Day: Time your visit so you'll be on the **Palatine Hill** at sunset, then head to **Enoteca Provincia Romana** for an aperitivo (5:30-7:30). This is an excellent wine bar that features wines and cuisine of the Lazio region, facing Trajan's column. (Via Foro Traiano 82, 066 994 0273, lunch reservations essential, closed Sunday and Monday for lunch, www.provinciaromana.it)

TIPS: *Don't go to the Forum between 10 and 2, the heaviest tourist times. The museums, on the other hand, are rarely crowded, and in addition to the Palazzo Nuovo, the Palatine Museum, with its mosaics and sculptures, is a good choice.*

TOURS

For the best guided small group tours, contact:
Context Travel at www.contexttravel.com.

RECOMMENDED READING

A Traveller in Rome by H. V. Morton

2 The Pietà, Saint Peter's Basilica

YOU'LL FEEL THE PULL of the greatest sculpture ever made as soon as you enter the doors of Saint Peter's. It's over there, to your right. Where cameras are flashing. Where tourists are posing. Where among the crowd there is at least one nun. Get close: the *Pietà*. *Pietà* means pity. And compassion.

Has compassion ever looked more beautiful? How did Michelangelo make marble flow? How did he capture such grace and serenity in Mary's face?

Michelangelo modeled the face of Mary after his mother: his mother who died when he was six.

He got all kinds of criticism for it. "Mary looks too young," people said. "If she has a thirty-three-year-old son, she's gotta be at least forty-five."

And Michelangelo said: "A woman so pure of body and soul is eternally young."

He was twenty-two, in 1498, when French Cardinal Jean de Bilheres, thinking ahead, commissioned Michelangelo to sculpt this image for his tomb. The Cardinal gave him 450 papal ducats. Not that Michelangelo cared much about money. He slept in his clothes in his studio; got his nose broken in drunken street brawls.

After he signed the contract, Michelangelo took off to Carrara in Tuscany to pick out the best piece of marble for the *Pietà*. He believed "Every block of stone has a statue inside it and it is the task of the sculptor to discover it."

Michelangelo was supposed to have the *Pietà* done in 1500, for the Holy Year. But when the pilgrims came through, he was still working on it. They stood back and watched Michelangelo free the statue from the stone. *Can you imagine?* They thought it was amazing—divine grace made flesh. They went back home spreading the word.

When it was finally unveiled, Michelangelo heard visitors saying he didn't sculpt it, that another artist, Gobbo di Milano, did. He got so enraged he snuck in late at night and carved his name onto Mary's sash. It was the only work he ever signed. He always regretted it.

This is one of the many masterpieces in Italy that may hold a memory for you of the first time you saw it. Maybe it was on a postcard or a slide in art history class.

For me, each time I see it in Rome, I'm pulled back to 1964, when the *Pietà* came to New York for the World's Fair. I lined up with the crowd, my mother behind me. The Vatican Pavilion!

We stepped onto a moving walkway. I heard a chorus singing "Alleluia, Alleluia." I felt my mother's hands on my shoulder. The room was draped in blue velvet with a sparkling light over the *Pietà*.

We floated by. It was the first A-R-T that I ever saw. I was seven, the age of reason. I wondered: How could something sad be beautiful? I heard gasps. I took a long look and reasoned: Beautiful.

Saint Peter's Basilica: Daily 7-6:30 (www.vatican.va)

⁊⁊

Golden Day: See the *Pietà* and the rest of the awe-inspiring **St. Peter's Basilica.** Have lunch at **Da Benito e Gilberto** (Via del Falco, 19, 06 686 7769, reservations recommended, closed Sunday), a cozy family run place that serves great fish. Or if your timing is such that a caffè or wine bar is the right choice, head to **Sorpasso** (Via Properzio 31-33, 06 8902 4554) or its nearby sister wine bar **Passaguai** (www.passaguai.it, Via Pomponio Leto 1, 06 8745 1358).

TIP: *Best to go in the afternoon, when the lines where you are screened to enter (like in airport security) are shorter. Avoid Wednesday mornings when there are Papal Audiences in the square.*

RECOMMENDED READING

A Journey into Michelangelo's Rome by Angela K. Nickerson

3 *Rome's Santa Maria Churches*

CHRISTIANS BEGAN TO OFFICIALLY call Mary "Mother of God" after the Council of Ephesus in 431 B.C. Devotion to her took hold in Rome, and goddesses' temples were abandoned or replaced with churches. Today, there are 26 churches in the Eternal City dedicated to Santa Maria, the Blessed Virgin Mary, *aka* BVM.

The grandest, largest, and oldest is the **Basilica Santa Maria Maggiore**, on the Esquiline Hill (near Termini). It was built over what was once a fertility temple, dedicated to Cybele, who Romans called *Magna Mater*—Great Mother. It's also called **The Madonna of the Snow**, because one summer night, on August 5, A.D. 359, Mary answered the prayer of Pope Liberius, who had asked for a sign of where to build a church, by miraculously bringing a snowfall to this hill, as if her answer was: "Right here!" Every year on August 5, white rose petals are released from the dome of the church to commemorate this event.

Inside the dazzling rectangular expanse, in the **Borghese Chapel**, is Rome's most important Marian icon: a Byzantine painting of the Virgin and Child, the *Salus Populi Romani*, **Protectress of the Roman People**, believed to have saved worshippers from the plague. The basilica ceilings are decorated with gold that came from the New World from Spain's Queen Isabella and King Ferdinand in the days of Christopher

Columbus. Marvelous fifth-century mosaics decorate the altar, further glorifying the BVM.

My favorite spot is the ***Loggia delle Benedizioni***, which you can see by winding around past the gift shop to the museum and requesting a guide, who, (for a small fee), will lead you upstairs to view amazing thirteenth-century mosaics that tell the story of the Madonna of the Snow. Grand baroque angel statues adorn this loggia, and the view from up here is stunning. Also, the guide is a member of the Vatican police—mine was a proud pope's body-guard—whose enthusiasm for the entire basilica was exhilarating: "Look at this!" he said, taking me around the corner of the loggia to see a circular staircase. "Bernini built this when he was only 16! Imagine how many popes have touched this railing!"

Basilica of Santa Maria Maggiore: Daily 7-7

Other favorite Santa Maria churches are:

Santa Maria and the Martyrs

No one will know what you're talking about if you call it this, except maybe a priest. Everybody else knows it as the **Pantheon**, a fantastic monument built to honor all the goddesses and gods. It was consecrated in the seventh century as a church dedicated to Mary and the martyrs.

The "Eye of God"—the humongous, uncovered circular opening at the top of the Pantheon's dome—frames the dramatic Roman sky, making the ever-changing city a part of this architectural wonder. It's fabulous near sunset. One winter I got there just before closing when a rosy cotton-candy-tinged-with-gold cloud floated across it, inspiring even one of the guards to throw his head back and sigh. And it's great in the rain. Especially in the rain, when water pours through and drains out the holes in its floor.

You also should take a moment to look at the plaque to the right of artist Raphael's tomb. On it is the name of the girl he was engaged to, Maria Bibbiena, his patron's niece. Raphael died at thirty-seven without ever marrying Maria. According to his biographer Vasari, he died from too much sex. Not with Maria, but with a baker's daughter who was his steady mistress.

Pantheon, aka Santa Maria and the Martyrs: Monday– Saturday 8:30-7:30, Sunday 9-6

Santa Maria Sopra Minerva

A zigzag away from the Pantheon takes you to this, Rome's only Gothic church. "Sopra" means "over," as the church was built over a place where there once was a temple complex devoted to Minerva (Goddess of Wisdom, Rome, and War), and Isis (Egyptian Goddess of Fertility).

I love Sopra Minerva's ceiling—a vaulted expanse of dreamy blue and stars, outlined in burgundy. There's a Renaissance **Chapel of the Annunciation**, where a willowy Mary, against a gold background, is handing out dowries to young maidens, just as the Dominican friars of this church once did. The master- piece here is the **Carafa Chapel**, painted by Filippino Lippi, where the BVM is surrounded by musical angels as she flies up to heaven. At the main altar is the **tomb of Saint Catherine of Siena**, a powerhouse of the fourteenth century who bravely fought to bring the Pope back to Rome from Avignon. And to the right of that main altar is Michelangelo's *Christ Carrying the Cross*—the cover over Jesus's privates is from Baroque days.

Santa Maria Sopra Minerva: Daily 8-7

Santa Maria in Cosmedin

This church, near the forum, wins for the best photo op, with the *Bocca della Verità* (Mouth of Truth) at its entrance, along with long lines of tourists unless you get there early or late in the day. The medieval legend of the big-faced disk says if a liar sticks his hand in its mouth, it'll get bitten off. Gregory Peck did a great job of faking his hand being eaten in *Roman Holiday*, and Audrey Hepburn's freaked-out yet charming reaction is a gem of a scene I replay on You Tube when I am Rome-sick.

Santa Maria in Cosmedin: Piazza della Bocca della Verità, daily 10-5

Santa Maria in Trastevere

You cross the Tiber, head through a maze of narrow streets, arrive at the piazza and BAM: topping this church is a vibrant mosaic frieze of Mary nursing Jesus, surrounded by ten lamp-holding virgins. This was built on a spot where it's believed oil spurted from the ground and flowed the entire day Jesus was born.

Over the inside altar, Mary's life story is told in Pietro Cavallini's thirteenth-century mosaics, culminating with her being crowned Queen of Heaven. It's best to get there on a sunny day, when the light bounces and sparkles off the gold background.

One of the most popular spots in the huge church is Saint Anthony's statue, surrounded by candles and covered with hand-scribbled notes, written to beg for miracles or help finding whatever's lost. At night the piazza surrounding this Santa Maria church gets magical. The lit-up mosaic makes it seem like Mary's

blessing the whole Felliniesque scene of tourists and locals passing through or hanging around the fountain. I can never resist
indulging in a caffè or Campari at the **di Marzio** to take it all in.

Santa Maria in Trastevere: Daily 7:30-9

Santa Maria della Pace

"Every moment is an opportunity for something wonderful to
happen," was the Baroque artists' philosophy. It's how I feel
when this church appears like a pearl tucked at the end of a
cobblestoned street in one of Rome's most theatrical settings.

Maybe I love della Pace so much because its opening hours
(see below) make it more elusive than the others—like an ultra-
handsome guy who's hardly ever available. When your timing is
right, you open the door to the small sanctuary and get a glorious blast of Raphael's frescos of four sibyls—prophetesses in
flowing robes, beautifully blending grace and power.

Sibyls were brilliant older women of Greece, Italy, and Persia
who studied the moon and the stars, predicting eclipses and creating the basis for astrology. Catholics adopted them, believing
Cumae (the sibyl on the left) predicted the birth of Christ. In
this painting, completed by Raphael's students after he died,
sibyls listen to the words of swooping angels.

To the left of that fresco is a chapel designed by Michelangelo,
and throughout the church are paintings of events of Mary's life,
from her birth to Assumption. Lots of female saints are honored
here as well, including Bridget and Catherine who border Mary
in the painting opposite Raphael's. Sculptures of Saints Cecilia,
Agnes, and Chiara adorn the arches.

Even if Santa Maria della Pace isn't open, you'll find another
treasure if you head left from the church's entrance: the

Bramante Cloister. This was the first work Bramante did in Rome, right before he went to work on Saint Peter's Square, and shows on a smaller scale his genius for harmony.

If you take the stairs from the cloister, you can peek through the bookshop window into the church for a view of Raphael's masterpiece, which takes the edge off disappointment if the sanctuary is closed.

Santa Maria della Pace: Vicolo del Arco della Pace 5, Monday and Friday 10-4, Tuesday-Thursday 9-12, closed Saturday and Sunday

ᴥ

Golden Day: Visit **Santa Maria Sopra Minerva** and then the **Pantheon** as the sun is setting. Have dinner at **Armando al Pantheon**, my favorite Rome restaurant. It's a cozy, family run place that serves delicious traditional dishes—such as *Spaghetti Cacio e Pepe*, with cheese and pepper, and *Abbacchio a scottadito*, baby lamb chops. (Salita de Crescenzi 31, 06 6880 3034, closed Saturday night and Sunday, reservations essential, www.armandoalpantheon.it)

TIP: *Roaming through the central areas of these churches during Mass times (Sunday mornings, early Saturday evenings) is not permitted, so arrange your visits accordingly.*

RECOMMENDED READING

A Catholic's Guide to Rome: Discovering the Soul of the Eternal City by Frank J. Korn

4 Rome's Churches Dedicated to Female Saints

WOMEN OF STEADFAST CONVICTION, who struggled, suffered, and triumphed in Rome, were elevated to sainthood and are remembered in churches all over the Eternal City.

Some are honored in tombs, such as **Saint Monica, Patron of Mothers**, who spent most of her life worrying about her ne'er-do-well son, Augustine. She lived to see him change his ways and is enshrined in the church named after him, **Sant' Agostino**.

My favorite churches dedicated to female saints are:

Saint Cecilia in Trastevere:
Patron Saint of Singers, Composers, and Musicians

A quiet Trastevere via opens to a large landscaped courtyard, which fronts this Basilica that was built over the home where Cecilia lived and died. Now the courtyard is a lovely neighborhood playground—where you're bound to see mammas circling strollers around the central Roman urn and nuns chatting away after mass.

In third-century Rome, Cecilia was known as the girl who heard angelic harmonies—she could play any instrument or sing any song. She secretly swore to be a chaste Christian, but went through with a marriage her parents arranged anyway. On the wedding night, she broke the news to her husband Valerian, telling him the only way he could touch her was to become a Christian, so he ran off to get baptized. When he returned, he found their bridal chamber transformed—full of flowers and his wife Cecilia wearing a crown of lilies and roses. This miracle swept Valerian into the faith. He made it his mission to help the poor and bury Christian martyrs and was beheaded for his belief.

Soon after, Cecilia was also tortured for her faith, forced into a tub of boiling water in her own bath tub. She sang all through the trial and miraculously survived, so a soldier was sent in to behead her. The three slashes of his sword didn't kill her immediately, but three days later, still singing, Cecilia died.

A marble sculpture of Cecilia in her death pose, with those three slashes on her neck, is set at the church's central altar. It was sculpted by Stefano Maderno, when her tomb was opened in 1595 and her body discovered in her death pose, miraculously not decomposed after 1,200 years.

Have a seat to admire the ninth-century mosaics above the altar, where Cecilia and husband Valerian are featured on the right of Christ, in regal Byzantine style. Downstairs there's an excavation, where you can see what's believed to have been Cecilia's home, and if you're lucky, you may get into the nineteenth century glittering Neo-Byzantine mosaic crypt, where Saint Agatha and Saint Agnes are honored along with Cecilia— otherwise take the chance to peek at it through the grating.

The most impressive attraction here is a thirteenth-century fresco of *The Universal Judgement* by Pietro Cavallini. It's behind the nun's choir loft, and the process of seeing it is a mini-adventure. From the outside of the church, you ring a buzzer to the left of the main entrance and are admitted into the Benedictine nun's convent. When I visited, I was met by the elderly, stooped

Sister Cecilia, (she of the wire-rimmed glasses and white hairs sprouting from her chin), who shuffled ahead of me into an elevator, escorted me to the loft, and then sat murmuring *Ave Marias* over her plastic rosary beads, as I had the joy of experiencing the fresco all to myself.

Cavallini's masterpiece had been covered by paneling and was rediscovered in the early 1900s. It's a glorious example of Roman naturalism that broke stiff Middle Ages form, beautifully expressing the profound emotions of Christ and the apostles, flanked by angels, elaborately winged, in shades of gold, rose, and sage. Art historians believe this was a major influence on Giotto, who went on to fresco the Scrovegni Chapel in Padua.

Santa Cecilia in Trastevere: Piazza Santa Cecilia, open daily 9:15-12:45, 4-6, Vespers daily at 7:15

TIP: *The Cavallini fresco in Saint Cecilia's can be viewed weekday mornings, 10-12:30, for 2.50 euro. There's a gift shop in the convent, where you can buy nun-made fruit jams and lavender sachets.*

Saint Agnes in Agone:
Patron Saint of Virgins and Girl Scouts

Don't let the word "Agone" make you think of "Agony" and keep you away from this glorious Borromini-designed structure that graces the Piazza Navona with its splendid curves and towers. "Agone" comes from the Latin "Campus Agonis," meaning "the site of competitions," which is what Piazza Navona was in the Middle Ages, when it was filled with water for boat races.

Soft Baroque music pipes through the ornate, dripping-with-gold church sanctuary. To the right of the altar is a statue of Saint Agnes, set against a pale blue background, with her arms outstretched and flames lapping at her feet. It was sculpted by a pupil of Bernini, and features Agnes in a breathtaking, transcendent moment.

Back in A.D. 304, men all over Rome were hot for beautiful thirteen-year-old Agnes, but she turned them away with her sweet smile, saying she was engaged to Jesus. "Let's strip her naked and have her walk to a whorehouse, that'll show her!" was the governor's idea to solve the problem. But miraculously, right where this church was built, Agnes' golden hair grew down to her
knees to cover her up, Lady Godiva style. Totally flummoxed by the cheerful virgin, the governor had her head cut off. A chapel to the left of the altar holds Agnes's shrunken head, in an ornate silver case.

The church is the perfect place to escape the Piazza Navona hubbub and one of the few left in Rome where you can light real candles.

Saint Agnes in Agone: Piazza Navona, open Monday–Friday 9:30-12:30, 3:30-7, Sunday and Holidays 9-1, 4-8 (www.santagneseinagone.org)

Church of Santa Brigida a Campo de' Fiori: Patron of Scholars and Sweden

If you get to this jewel-box between four and five in the afternoon, you'll hear nuns singing vespers in sweet harmonies. They're Brigittines, the best-dressed sisters in Rome, with long gray habits and tight headpieces accented by a white band and shining red studs. They belong to an order founded in the fourteenth century by Saint Bridget of Sweden, aka The Mystic of the North.

Bridget's famous visions started coming to her when she was just a girl. She married when she was fourteen and had eight children. When her husband died, Bridget was forty-two, and she decided to follow her childhood visions by founding an order of nuns. The monastery she built became a Swedish literary center (thus her scholarly patron side) because she allowed her holy assistants to have as many books as they wanted.

Bridget came to Rome in 1349 for two reasons. One, she wanted the Pope to approve her order, and two, she'd had a vision that he'd die soon, so she thought she should tell him. She met the Pope, he approved the Brigittines and then (true to Bridget's prophecy), he died four months later. Bridget stayed in Rome, living near what is now her church, and died there at the age of seventy-one.

Bridget's convent, around the corner from her church, is now the **Casa di Santa Brigida guesthouse**, run by her nuns. The downstairs rooms where the saint lived are furnished with dark antiques and elegant draperies, and the rooftop terrace has amazing views.

The roof of Saint Bridget's church is graced with baroque statues of Bridget and her daughter, Saint Catherine. Inside it's prettily done up in rust-colored marble and gold moldings, with frescos telling Bridget's life story. It's located right on the Michelangelo-designed Piazza Farnese, which features fountains made from tubs taken from the Baths of Caracalla, the harmonious façade of the Palazzo Farnese, and handsome priests passing by on their way to Vatican City.

Church of Santa Brigida a Campo de' Fiori: Piazza Farnese (www.brigidine.org)

ᕱᕇ

Golden Day: Get to **Saint Bridget's** between 4 and 5 P.M. to hear vespers. Have a caffè or aperitivo at the **Caffè Farnese**, and a traditional budget Roman dinner at **Ai Balestrari** (Via dei Balestrari 41, closed Monday), or for something pricier, but always delicious, reserve a table at **Roscioli** which is also a wine shop, bakery, and deli. (Via dei Giubbonari 21/22, 06 687 5287, closed Sunday, www.salumeriaroscioli.com)

TIP: *Casa di Santa Brigida guesthouse is one of the best bargain accommodations in the historic center. Location is tops, rooms are simple but comfy. Reservations must be made far in advance: www.brigidine.org.*

RECOMMENDED READING

Saints Preserve Us! by Sean Kelly and Rosemary Rogers

The Pilgrim's Italy: A Travel Guide to the Saints by James and Colleen Heater

5 Catacombs of Priscilla

THE WORLD'S OLDEST IMAGE of the Blessed Virgin Mary (from A.D. 230) is painted on the wall of these catacombs, that all began with a wealthy woman named Priscilla. She was the wife of a Roman Consul, who was executed in A.D. 91 for atheism—that is, he didn't believe in Roman gods, but was a follower of Christianity. While Romans practiced cremation, Christians believed in the resurrection, so they wrapped their dead in linen without embalming them and had to find space outside the city walls for burials.

Priscilla had her husband buried on a part of the family's land that was once a quarry and generously donated the property for other Christian families to use. Between the second and fourth centuries, the spot turned into eight miles of layered tunnels, lined with shelves of tombs, and punctuated by larger *cubicule* (caves), that were elaborately decorated for the wealthier folk.

Popes and martyrs were buried here, and it became known as The Queen of the Catacombs. When Emperor Constantine legalized Christianity in A.D. 313, it still was used for burials, but also became a pilgrimage site for the devout, who made a ritual of having picnics down here, to be near their heroes and beloved family members.

It's a cool, eerie experience to wander through the labyrinth that was once full of beautifully carved marble sarcophagi and slabs, funerary statues, and frescos. Lots of the treasures disappeared when Rome was invaded in the sixth and seventh centuries, then also when the tombs were discovered by archaeologists in the sixteenthth century, and again when they were rediscovered by travelers on the Grand Tour, as those eighteenth-century visitors had no qualms about hauling off free souvenirs. Still, the mysterious atmosphere, remaining wall paintings, along with the new museum upstairs, inspires fascination.

Besides the precious image of Mary nursing Jesus, there is an impressive underground Greek Chapel, painted with Pompeii style early Christian symbols (doves, fish, anchors), and arches featuring Jesus as the Good Shepherd and Jonah and the whale.

I'm drawn to a fresco in the Cubicle of Velata, where a woman in a ruby red robe stands with her arms outstretched, and another in the Greek Chapel, a Banquet of the Eucharist, showing women celebrating. These two caused much hoopla in 2013, when the site had a grand opening of its new museum and restored artifacts. Catholic women who've been fighting for female ordination claimed that the images were clearly signs that there were women priests in those early days...*so why were they being denied that right in the new millennium?* Vatican authorities retaliated, claiming that the woman with outstretched arms was a traditional image from pagan and early Christian art, called an "Orans," from the Latin word for "praying," and certainly not a priestess. The debate rages on!

Compared to the Appian Way catacombs, the Priscilla Catacombs attract fewer tourists, giving you a chance to experience this unique piece of history in a more tranquil setting. It's run by Benedictine nuns, a cheerful bunch in black habits, who follow the order's motto: "Pray and Work." They're busy gals, running the gift shop, hand painting reproduction plaques of the catacomb wall paintings, and proudly making priests' vestments.

The 2013 restoration brings a hi-tech angle to the place, with glass floors that allow you to see the layers of the underground— the top layer is the oldest, then they kept digging as more graves were needed. Also, Google Maps created a virtual tour of the entire complex, for armchair travelers.

Catacombs of Priscilla: open 8:30-12, 2:30-7, closed Monday, 06 862 06272 (www.catacombepriscilla.com)
Museo di Priscilla: www.mupris.net

⚶

Golden Day: Taxi over to the **Catacombs of Priscilla** (about ten minutes from the center). Tours in English run regularly and last about a half hour—you can call to find out that day's schedule or just show up and there may be a half-hour wait for the next tour to start, giving you time to visit the museum. For lunch nearby, go to **La Mora**, a folksy place that serves excellent Tuscan cuisine, such as fettucine with mushrooms or roasted beef and potatoes. (Piazza Crati 13, 06 862 06613, closed Monday and Wednesday lunch, www.lamora.it)

TIP: *Bring a sweater, it's cold down there!*

RECOMMENDED READING

The Art of the Roman Catacombs by Gregory S. Athnos

6 Bernini's Beautiful Broads and the Galleria Borghese

YOU'D THINK THE ARTIST WHO SCULPTED the Fountain of the Four Rivers in Piazza Navona, the Triton in the Piazza Barberini, and Saint Peter's flamboyant altar would have been a wild man. But actually Gian Lorenzo Bernini took on his masterpiece work like a monk, sculpting seven hours a day, up until his death at eighty-one. He poured all his passion into his creations—sculptures of figures caught in theatrical moments that absolutely define baroque Rome.

Bernini did have one enticing affair, with Constanza Bonarelli, the wife of one of his assistants. Things heated up when Constanza started to fool around with Bernini's younger brother. Bernini flew into a violent rage, threatening to throw acid on Constanza's face. Then he turned to beating up that younger brother, until the Pope stepped in to put a stop to the whole deal. Bernini's *Constanza* bust is in the Bargello in Florence. With her lips slightly parted and blouse unbuttoned, it seems as though she was sculpted just a moment before she and Bernini jumped into bed for a good time.

Bernini calmed down after Constanza, married at forty-one, and fathered eleven kids. His daily routine was morning mass at the Gesu, work-work-work, and then back to church where he prayed with the Jesuits.

Unlike Michelangelo's sculptures (such as the *Pieta* and *David*) that have a powerful meditative style, Bernini's creations seem to be formed in wax. Their robes flow, they laugh, scream, sigh, and pulse with vitality.

On the **Ponte Sant'Angelo** you'll be surrounded by the dramatic angels he designed. And in these sculptures, you'll see how Bernini captures women in climactic moments...literally:

● *Ecstasy of Saint Teresa*, **1647-1652** (Santa Maria della Vittoria, Via XX Settembre 17, near Termini)
It looks like the Carmelite Spanish nun Bernini placed in a stage set altar is having quite an "ecstasy" as an angel pierces her with a golden shaft.

Saint Teresa had loads of mystical visions, and wrote that this piercing left her "on fire with the love of God" and "The pain was so great that it made me moan; and yet so surpassing was the sweetness of this excessive pain that I could not wish to be rid of it." Clearly, Bernini's genius took Teresa's account and ran with it.

● *Beata Ludovica Albertoni*, **1671-1674** (San Francesco a Ripa, Piazza San Francesco d'Assisi 88, Trastevere)
Here the mystic Ludovica is sprawled out in bed with her head thrown back as she clutches her breast. Some say she's in her death throes, but since she has her shoes on, others believe Bernini caught her in a private, earth-shattering, "seeing the Divine" pose. It's best to visit the church in the morning when sunlight streams over Ludovica from the cupola above.

Visit **The Galleria Borghese**, a splendid museum to see these Bernini masterpieces:

* *Daphne and Apollo, 1622-1625* (Room III)
   The virgin water nymph manages a fantastic escape from Apollo by transforming into a laurel tree before your eyes. Her hair and fingertips become leaves, her feet and ankles the tree trunk.

* *Pluto and Proserpina, 1621-1622* (Room IV)
   A teardrop runs down Proserpina's face as she smushes her hand into Pluto's chin, fighting him off with a heaven-help-me look. Pluto scoops her up and gets a firm grab on her thigh. The three-headed barking dog adds to the drama.

   This is Bernini's version of the Greek myth that told how Pluto, God of the Underworld, got wowed by the beautiful Goddess of Vegetation he saw picking flowers in a field, and swooped up to kidnap her.

Other fabulous women in the Borghese are:

* *Venus Victrix, 1805-1808* (Room I)

   Here's Pauline Bonaparte (Napoleon's sister) posed regally as the nude goddess. Pauline came to Rome as a ravishing twenty-three-year-old widow, won the heart of Prince Borghese, married him, and became mistress of the Villa. It caused quite a scandal when Pauline stripped to

model for the sculptor Canova, and her prince husband kept this statue hidden away while he was alive. Pauline's only comment on the affair was, "The room was well heated." Famously vain woman that she was, Pauline was also known to have used her servants as footstools and liked to have, in her words, "a large Negro" carry her to her bath.

- ***Sacred and Profane Love*, 1805-1808 (Room XX)**
Painted by Titian when he was just twenty-five for a Venetian nobleman's marriage, the Venuses here are named differently from what you'd expect. The Profane Venus is in proper Renaissance dress, drawing a pot of gold to her side, signifying "fleeting earthly happiness." The Sacred Venus is naked, holding an eternal flame, meaning "eternal happiness in heaven." She wears only her magic girdle, which gave her the power to attract her many lovers.

Galleria Borghese: 8:30-7:30, closed Monday, 06 841 3979 (www.galleriaborghese.it)

Golden Day: Plan on a **picnic in the Borghese Gardens** before or after your visit to the **Galleria Borghese**. You can gather your own goodies at an *alimenatri*, deli—there are good places near Campo dei Fiori, such as **Roscioli** (Via dei Chiavari 34, www.salumeriaroscioli.com), or to have it all done for you, go to **GiNa**, right near the entrance to the Borghese Gardens, where they provide you with picnic baskets and a delicious selection of panini and salads. (Via San Sebastianello 7/A, 06 678 0251, www.ginaroma.com)

TIP: *Reservations for the Galleria Borghese are a must; you can make them easily by phone or online. This turns out to be a good thing, because you get to browse without crowds.*

RECOMMENDED READING

Bernini's Beloved: A Portrait of Costanza Piccolomini by Sarah McPhee

7 Villa Farnesina

LE DELIZIE OR "THE DELIGHTS" was the original name of this villa, known back in Renaissance days as the best party house in Rome. It was built by Agostino Chigi, banker to the popes, aka the Richest Man in the World. Way before Chigi got to it, on the same site in 44 B.C., Cleopatra had carried on with Julius Caesar in a villa the emperor had here.

Chigi was a generous patron of the arts, so in 1506 he called in the top architect (Baldassarre Peruzzi) and best painters to create luscious gardens and a villa packed with frescos of mythological love scenes to inspire his guests. Spectacles with singers and dancers were staged here, followed by opulent banquets. For the grand finale, Chigi had his servants toss his used china and silverware into the Tiber. Little did his guests know he kept a net down there to catch it all.

The stars of Chigi's parties were Rome's adored courtesans. These beautiful ladies, called "honest prostitutes," in addition to providing their expected services, could recite classical poetry at the drop of a hat and serenade their admirers with lutes or violins. They were treated well by Rome's many wealthy bachelors, who ranged from merchant traders to priests. Like movie stars, when courtesans rode through the streets in their fancy carriages, people would run out to gawk at their elegant get-ups, jewels, and hairstyles.

Imperia, one of Rome's most famous courtesans, was a favorite of Chigi's—he planned on living with her in this villa when he first decided to build it. The painter Raphael, who also spent quality time with Imperia, had her model for  one of the first frescos you'll see here in the *Loggia of Galatea*.

The image of the half-naked sea nymph (surprisingly muscular and fleshy) is a scene from a Greek myth that began with the Cyclops Polyphemus falling madly in love with Galatea. Unfortunately for Polyphemus, Galatea fell in love with a mortal shepherd, Acis. When Polyphemus saw the two of them cavorting, he flipped out and threw a boulder at the couple, killing Acis. The blood of Galatea's dead lover turned into a river that she rides away on in this painting, triumphantly escaping Polyphemus.

Raphael's model Imperia was not so triumphant. The courtesan had many men besides Chigi, and fell in love with one of them. When he tired of her, Imperia feared she was losing her beauty, and at the age of twenty-six swallowed poison and died. The exact date of her suicide was August 15 (coincidentally, the celebration of Mary's Assumption into heaven). There was a huge storm in Rome that night, with folks in the city saying Jupiter had thundered down to take away their beloved beauty.

Imperia's image appears again upstairs in this villa, where the artist Sodoma frescoed Chigi's bedroom with scenes from the life of Alexander the Great. There *The Wedding of Alexander and*

Roxane reeks with sexual anticipation, as Roxane's clothes are tugged at by *putti* and Alexander stands awaiting his bride.

Chigi and Imperia had broken up before her suicide, and he'd gone to Venice and gotten himself another courtesan, Francesca. The couple moved in here and, after having four children, the Pope insisted Chigi marry Francesca. Their wedding was one of the biggest bashes ever held in the villa, with Pope Leo and twelve cardinals in attendance.

For all the great parties at Le Delizie, guests would enter through the *Loggia of Psyche*, the villa's most beautiful setting, which originally opened to the gardens and wasn't enclosed like it is today. Raphael designed it, but had no time to paint it, as he was busy with other jobs and his romance with Margherita Luti, a baker's daughter who lived in the neighborhood. His students completed it, bringing in elements of nature with ornamentation of lush greenery, flowers, and fruit surrounding frescos that tell the love story of Amore and Psyche. Here's a myth that fit right in with the Renaissance philosophy of joining the Divine (Amore) with the Mortal Mind/Soul (Psyche). The goddess Venus is of course involved, and after many trials, the main characters are united in a marriage celebration painted on the ceiling.

After Chigi's death, the Farnese family bought Le Delizie, renamed it Farnesina, and planned on connecting it to their palazzo near the Campo dei Fiori. The proposed bridge was never completed, but part of it forms that beautiful, dripping-with-vines archway you'll see over the Via Giulia.

Villa Farnesina: Via della Lungara 230, open Monday-Saturday, 9-2 (www.villafarnesina.it)

༄ঌ

Golden Day: Visit the **Farnesina**, then lunch at **da Gildo** to enjoy simple Roman specialties on the outside terrace, such as *vignarola*, vegetable stew, a springtime treat. (Via della Scala 31, 06 580 0733, closed Thursday)

TIP: *This is one of the few museums in Rome that is open on Monday.*

RECOMMENDED READING

Raphael: A Passionate Life by Antonio Forcellino

Palazzo Barberini

In *ROMAN HOLIDAY*, THE PRINCESS PLAYED by Audrey Hepburn escapes from this palace to end up on a romantic adventure with reporter Gregory Peck. It's sublime to play Audrey's moves backward and escape inside the Barberini to peacefully take in Renaissance masterpieces.

The palace was the digs of Maffeo Barberini, who transformed it when he became Pope Urban VIII in 1623. He went all out to make it *splendido*, calling in the best artists of the day, including Bernini and Borromini. You'll climb Borromini's spiral staircase as you enter. Inside you'll get a dizzying hit looking up at the Grand Salone ceiling, frescoed by Pietro Da Cortona. Go ahead and lie back on a couch to admire this *Triumph of Providence*, where golden bees (the Barberini family emblem) ascend to the heavens.

Most of the rooms you'll be walking through were originally the apartment of Princess Anna Colonna Barberini, who had married the pope's nephew. She was the palace hostess and the most powerful woman in Rome during the Barberini's seventeenth-century heyday. The family's fortunes got dispersed over the years, and the palace was sold to the State in 1949, becoming the National Gallery of Art.

In the galleries, you'll see beautiful women immortalized by masters, including:

❀ *Fornarina* (Raphael's Girlfriend)

The subject of Raphael's most famous portrait is his longtime lover, Margherita Luti, who he called Fornarina, which translates to "little oven." The dark-haired, bare-breasted, mischievous-looking beauty was a Trastevere baker's daughter. She wears a bracelet with Raphael's signature on it, as if they were going steady.

❀ *Beatrice Cenci* (Who Murdered Her Daddy)

With those legendary huge eyes and innocent over-the-shoulder look, it's hard to imagine this sixteen-year-old bludgeoned her father to death. That is until you hear the story of the man's atrocious cruelty to his whole family, who joined Beatrice in the murder. The painting is believed to have been completed the night before Beatrice was decapitated, in front of huge crowds on the Ponte Sant'Angelo. It's attributed to Guido Reni, but many believe Elisabetta Sirani, a female artist, is the one who painted it.

❀ *Judith Beheading Holofernes* (Bible's Gutsiest Widow)

Master painter Caravaggio captures a gory biblical moment here. It's Judith, chopping off the head of General Holofernes, complete with spurting blood. Her maid stands by with a "Take that, you bastard!" look.

According to the Old Testament, Judith was a widow who got fed up with her Israeli countrymen in their fight against the Assyrians, so she took matters into her own hands, got all dolled up, and went to visit the enemy's General Holofernes. Clever woman that she was, Judith promised him helpful information and sexual favors, which she never made good on. The general lusted after Judith, and threw a banquet where he became "sodden with wine," expecting some nooky afterward. Imagine his surprise when Judith snuck into his tent, found Holofernes sprawled out drunk as a skunk, and lopped his head off.

Caravaggio's brilliant brush strokes illuminate Judith's conflicted expression. She's repulsed, curious, a bit repentant, but committed. For his model, he used one of Rome's most popular courtesans of the day, Fillide Melandroni. A few years after the painting was completed, Caravaggio got into a street brawl with Melandroni's "protector," Ranuccio Tomassoni. It's believed Caravaggio was trying to castrate Tomassoni, but instead gave his thigh a fatal artery-severing slash. Caravaggio was exiled from Rome for the murder, never to return.

Palazzo Barberini: Via delle Quattro Fontane 13, 8:30–7, closed Monday (www.galleriaborghese.it)

❧

Golden Day: Morning at the **Barberini** and lunch at **Colline Emiliane** for specialties of the Emilia-Romagna region—the lasagna and *tagliatelle alla bolognese* are out of this world. (Via degli Avignonesi, 22, 06 481 7538, reservations essential, closed Sunday night and Monday)

TIP: *Don't miss the classic garden in the back of the museum.*

RECOMMENDED READING

The Families Who Made Rome: A History and Guide by Anthony Majanlahti
Beatrice's Spell: The Enduring Legacy of Beatrice Cenci by Belinda Jack

9 *Palazzo Colonna*

EVERY SATURDAY MORNING, the Colonnas (Rome's most illustrious family), host a spectacular open house, welcoming visitors to the downstairs salons of their palazzo. They still live on the upper floors, but since the seventeenth century they've been regularly showing off their wealth and power to the awestruck public. Don't be surprised if you see a Colonna prince milling about. When I was last there, I got distracted by a smiling *signor* in a well-tailored suit, who stood apart, surveying the scene. "That was Don Prospero," my tour guide reverently whispered, as we moved on to the next dazzling room.

The Colonna's *piano nobile* was remodeled in the days of the Palace of Versailles. It's an explosion of Baroque: dramatic ceiling murals bursting with smiling *putti* and flowers, enormous Murano glass chandeliers, tapestries, gilded mirrors, Greek statues, a majestic throne room built for the fifteenthth-century Colonna Pope, Marco V. The masterpiece painting collection includes Annibale Carracci's *The Beaneater*—a hilarious contrast to the gorgeousness, featuring a peasant hovered over his bowl of beans, who Van Gogh later used for inspiration.

The family shouts out their nine centuries of triumph with their crest (a column) all over the place, along with paintings of their superhero ancestor, Marcantonio II, who in 1571 led the papal fleet to win the Battle of Lepanto. This was a key battle in

European history—the Ottoman Empire was defeated off the coast of Greece, making Christians victorious over Muslim rule. You'll see Marcantonio on the ceiling in combat, being crowned by the Virgin, entering into heaven.

The Great Hall is the climax of all the opulence, where visitors of yesteryear would greet the resident Colonna nobility, honoring them as though they were goddesses and gods. This is also where the last scene of *Roman Holiday* was shot—where Princess Audrey presides at a press conference in one of cinema's most poignant scenes, followed by Gregory Peck walking away, alone in this expanse, transformed into a man of integrity.

Let's focus on some of the extraordinary, courageous Colonna women who are celebrated here:

Vittoria Colonna (1490-1547)
Beloved by Michelangelo/Renaissance Poetess

Vittoria's portrait hangs in the upper level of the Great Hall. She's dressed in green silk, with a widow's headdress and penetrating gaze. She was married off to an army captain, who was often away in battle, inspiring her to hone her love-letter writing skills. When she was 35, he died of a war injury. Instead of following the traditional widow's route—joining a nunnery or having her family arrange yet another advantageous marriage to further the Colonna line—Vittoria dedicated herself to writing poetry. She hosted artists' and writers' salons at a castle in Ischia and then in Rome, where she preferred holding court at the Convent of San Silvestro, rather than this family palazzo. It was in Rome where an intense life-long, platonic friendship between Vittoria and Michelangelo took hold. The two read

Dante together, wrote poems to each other, and became followers of the Oratory of Divine Love, a humanist group that was
seeking church reform.

Continuing to the **Princess Isabelle apartments**, you'll
discover...

Marie Mancini (1639-1715)
Seventeenth-Century Feminist

Marie is the ravishing dark-eyed beauty you'll find in the Sala
del Baldacchino. She was one of five gorgeous Mancini sisters,
who (after the death of their aristocratic father) were brought
from Rome to France by their shrewd mother. With their exotic
Mediterranean looks, the Mancini girls caused a sensation
amongst Parisians. Marie became the first love of Louis XIV,
aka The Sun King, who showered her with jewels and affection.
Sadly, Marie's mother and Louis's mother did not see this bond
as a good thing, so Marie was shipped back to Rome and married
off to a Colonna: Prince Lorenzo Onofrio.

The union began joyfully—Marie bore three children and
brought her love of the French decorative arts to inspire the
floral room here. She and hubby Lorenzo were beloved for
their hosting of colorful balls at the palazzo. But at the elev-
en-year-marriage point, in 1672, she'd had enough of Lorenzo's
philandering. In a jealous rage, she left Rome, teamed up with
her glamorous sister Hortense, and the two set off defying their
husbands, as adventurous ladies, kind of a seventeenth-century
Thelma and Louise. They publically took on lovers, and sometimes disguised themselves as men, gambling, and becoming
tabloid sensations. When Marie's money ran out, she wrote and
sold her memoirs, to ensure that her true story be told.

Isabelle Sursock Colonna (1889-1984), Italy's Alternate Queen

The apartments are named for this family heroine, a Lebanese banking heiress who married into the Colonna family in 1909. Black and white photos of Isabelle can be found in her lavish reception rooms, where she appears as a formidable figure, dressed in stiff brocade with an impeccably styled hairdo. Isabelle arrived here as a Colonna bride when wars began to rage, and she deftly helped to steer the family to take its right place amidst Rome's political and papal worlds. A woman who lived her convictions, she stood up against the Nazis and sheltered Jews here during World War II.

Princess Isabelle was fiercely committed to preserving this place and lived here until her death in 1984. I am especially grateful to her for the room of the Vanvitelli landscapes collection. They're charming, detailed renditions of what Rome looked like in the eighteenth century—that is the Tiber without its embankments, the Trinita dei Monti before there were Spanish Steps. It opens me up to yet another layer of this amazing city, reminding me that places I love here have been beloved eternally.

Galleria Colonna: Piazza SS Apostoli 66, open Saturdays only, 9-1:15, tours in English offered at 11:45 (www.galleriacolonna.it)

❧

Golden Day: After your Galleria Colonna visit, an obvious dining choice may be **Open Colonna**, a chic Michelin-starred restaurant on the rooftop of the **Palazzo delle Espozioni**, (Via

Milano 9a, 06 478 22641, closed Sunday and Monday nights, www.opencolonna.it), that offers a low-priced brunch buffet. If you'd like something more traditional, head to the nearby Monti neighborhood's **La Taverna dei Fiori Imperiali**, a family-run place that serves up classic Roman pastas, seasonal specialties, and delicious desserts. (Via della Madonna dei Monti 9, 06 679 8643, closed Tuesday, www.latavernadeiforiimperiali.com)

TIP: *It costs fifteen euros extra to tour the Princess Isabella apartments, with the option offered after the main thirty-minute tour. Tickets must be purchased in cash, so come prepared.*

RECOMMENDED READING

The Kings' Mistresses: The Liberated Lives of Marie Mancini, Princess Colonna, and Her Sister Hortense, Duchess Mazarin by Elizabeth C. Goldsmith

10 *Taste Rome*

INDULGING IN LONG, STRETCHED OUT Roman meals is following a tradition that's been going on here since ancient times. So go ahead and immerse yourself in the Eternal City's bold, vibrant flavors. Traditional dishes to order are:

- **Pasta**: *Cacio e Pepe* (with pecorino cheese and pepper), *Carbonara* (guanciale, egg, and cheese), *Amatriciana* (guanciale, tomato, and cheese)
- **Vegetables**: *Carciofi* (Artichokes—either alla Giudia, fried, or alla Romana, braised), *Puntarelle* (a variety of chicory, served with an anchovy/garlic dressing)
- **Meat**: *Straccetti di Manzo con Rughetta* (strips of beef with arugula), *Saltimbocca* (veal with prosciutto and sage), *Coda alla Vaccinara* (oxtail stew), *Abbacchio* (baby lamb)

Favorite Restaurant

- **Armando al Pantheon,** Salita de Crescenzi 31, 06 6880 3034, closed Saturday night and Sunday, reservations essential (www.armandoalpantheon.it)
  The location, steps from the Pantheon, is perfect. The atmosphere is always welcoming, and the family here has been making my every visit to Rome delicious for decades. I count

on them for my ideal Welcome Back to Rome meal: *Cacio e Pepe, Abbacchio a scottadito* ... always extraordinary.

Favorite Caffès

* **Antico Caffè Greco,** Via Condotti 86 (near Spanish Steps, www.anticocaffegreco.eu)

This ultra-elegant spot was founded by a Greek signor in 1760, thus the name. Amidst the waiters in crisp white jackets, marble tables, and gilded mirrors, check out the photo of Buffalo Bill, whose 1906 visit caused a sensation. Worth the splurge to take a break from Via Condotti window shopping.

* **Antico Caffè della Pace,** Via della Pace 3 (near Piazza Navona, www.caffedellapace.it)

  From 1891, you'll discover a theatrical atmosphere here—both in the interior dark wood bar and on the patio flanked by ivy-covered walls. In the evenings it becomes a hipster gathering spot. Remember Julia Roberts sitting here in *Eat Pray Love*?

Best Coffee (Near the Pantheon)

These two old school spots offer excellent coffee, with limited seating, as most come for a quick pick me up at the counter or to buy beans to bring home:

* **Caffè Sant'Eustachio,** Piazza Sant'Eustachio 82 (www.santeustachioilcaffe.it)

  Many claim they serve the best cappuccino in Rome.

❋ **Tazza D'Oro,** Via degli Orfani 84
(www.tazzadorocoffeeshop.com)
They make a great *granita di caffè*—iced espresso with whipped
cream.

Gelato

❋ **Giolitti,** Via degli Uffici del Vicario 40 (near the Pantheon)
It's old fashioned and full of tourists, but I still love the elegant atmosphere and the fruit flavors, slathered with *panna*
(cream), doled out by smiling servers.

❋ **Gelateria del Teatro,** Via di San Simone 70 (near Piazza
Navona)
Tucked in a charming alley off Via Coronari, here owners
Stefano and Silvia whip up delicious classic flavors (pistachio
and dark chocolate), along with unique creations (lavender
or sesame), as well as dairy-free sorbets.

❋ **Old Bridge,** Viale Bastioni di Michelangelo (Vatican City)
Stop by here for generous scoopage *con panna* (with whipped
cream) and fantastic flavors, conveniently located between
the Vatican Museums and Saint Peter's Basilica.

Chocolate

❋ **Moriondo & Gariglio,** Via del Piè di Marmo 21-22 (near
the Pantheon)
This fairy tale–styled shop near the Pantheon was founded by
a family from Turin over a hundred years ago. Sales *signorine*
wear old-fashioned lace caps and box up bon-bons, marzi-
pans, or fruit glaces into beautifully crafted boxes at an old
world pace…so don't say I didn't warn you.

Bakeries

* **Forno,** Campo dei Fiori 22, open 7:30–2:30, 4:30–8
  (www.fornocampodefiori.com)
  Be prepared to get in line for the legendary *pizza bianca* (white
  pizza)—and they also make great focaccia, *pignoli* (pine nut)
  cookies, and fruit tarts.

* **Valzani,** Via del Moro 37, Trastevere, closed Monday and
  Tuesday mornings
  A sweet Roman institution since 1925, specializing in *torta sacher*,
  and also offering goodies made with dried fruits and nuts.

Wine Bars

In ancient Rome there were *enoteche* at every corner, but as the
city transformed, the tradition slipped away. In the 1970s a wine
bar revival began in the Eternal City. These days, *enoteche* fill up
with working people meeting friends after a long day. Along
with your wine, you'll enjoy such delicious Roman treats as *suppli*
(deep-fried rice croquettes stuffed with cheese) or pecorino
cheese wrapped in chestnut leaves.

* **L'Angolo Divino**, Via dei Balestrari 12, closed Monday
  A romantic spot behind the Campo de' Fiori clamor, where
  you can get great snacks like *tuna carpaccio* or a delicious meal
  by candlelight along with choice, reasonably priced wines.

* **Il Goccetto**, Via dei Banchi Vecchi 14, open noon–2,
  6–midnight, closed Sunday
  It's always packed with locals, many filtering out to the sidewalk, aka the smoking section. Order up at the front counter,

then tuck yourself into the cozy backroom, and have owner Sergio pair a cheese plate to match your wine.

* **Cul de Sac,** Piazza di Pasquino 73 (near Piazza Navona)
One of the first of the new wave of Roman wine bars, this place has a list of 1,500 vintages. Get there before 9 p.m. to score an outside table and order a variety of housemade pâtés—a specialty they do well.

* **Vino Roma**, Via in Selci, 84G (between Colosseum and Termini, www.vinoroma.com)
Charming sommelier Hande Leimer and her team host tastings and events to educate travelers from around the world about Italian wines. Tastings are offered in English, German, Japanese, Italian, and Turkish. Offerings include wine and cheese lunches and Wine Wednesdays that focus on different themes.

RESOURCES FOR FOOD IN ROME

Aglio, Olio e Peperoncino: www.aglioolioepeperoncino.com
Elizabeth Minchilli in Rome: www.elizabethminchilliinrome. com, and her EatRome App
Parla Food: www.parlafood.com, and Katie Parla's Rome App
Tavole Romane: www.tavoleromane.com
The Rome Digest: www.theromedigest.com

RECOMMENDED READING

Williams-Sonoma Rome by Maureen Fant

11 Cooking with Daniela del Balzo

THE DIVINE AROMA OF PEPPERS cooking in olive oil and garlic fills Daniela del Balzo's kitchen. Six of us American travelers in Rome are hovering around her stove, sipping prosecco, nibbling bruschetta, stirring and chopping, under Daniela's enthusiastic guidance. Her one-day cooking class is a lovely respite from the tourist treadmill of the bustling Eternal City. Today we've slowed down from visiting monuments and museums and are immersing ourselves in the heart and soul of the culinary traditions of Rome.

Daniela is a mamma-to-all type *signora*, who sets up her class as though she's taking us along with her for a typical Roman day: shopping at the local market and cooking in her apartment. Her passion for cooking is boundless. She learned the traditional way—from her mother, grandmother, and great-grandmother, during her childhood in Naples. Then, after a twenty-year career working for *Alitalia*, she decided to go back to school to focus on her love for cooking. She studied at Italy's renowned Gambero Rosso Cooking School, the French Culinary Arts School & Le Cordon Bleu, and the International Cooking School of Naples. Now she teaches from her home on Rome's Aventine Hill. She's married to a Roman, has a mother-in-law who lives two floors above her, and two 20-something sons—one who has also become a chef, following in her footsteps. Putting all these work and life experiences together, Daniela has created a program where she teaches Roman classics with professional flair, always adding a Neapolitan touch from her ancestors.

The class begins before lunch in the bustling Testaccio market. Rome's slaughterhouse was once located here, and Testaccio became famous for its restaurants that featured quality meat dishes and Roman specialties from the *quinto quarto* (fifth quarter), meaning what's left of the animal after butchering—oxtails, tripe, pajata (calf intestines), etc. Lately the neighborhood has become, as the Italians say, "trendy," with clubs and hot spots, but discovering it with Daniela is the ideal way to connect with its roots.

She's been shopping in Testaccio for years, and everywhere we go it feels like we're tagging along with her on a family visit. I can't help but compare my Los Angeles supermarket style— which involves rushing around with my cart, not speaking to a soul—to Daniela's. With this *signora*, every encounter is leisurely and personal. The vendors ask about her sons, she tells them her cooking plans for the day, and then there's serious teamwork to pick out the best peppers. Next there's an intense discussion with her handsomest of butchers about the right amount of veal for lunch—and by the way, ladies, Daniela's butcher is a major attraction of the market! The excursion is a sensory treat—we're surrounded by abundant displays of deep green chicory, glistening anchovies, the first strawberries of spring.

We move on to Daniela's apartment—a sophisticated, sunlit place, with cozy family antiques. Fun begins in the kitchen, where we tie on aprons, and learn as we go, to Daniela's free-flowing teaching style. Her recipes are simple, but by watching her, we learn subtle techniques for bringing out the best flavors of the market's ingredients. There's the way to jiggle the pan to cook up *saltimbocca*—which translates to "jump in your mouth," because the taste of the veal/prosciutto/sage combo is so lively. There's an extra step in her *peperonata* recipe—covering the pan with a domed lid after sautéing, just before baking, so the result is a perfectly soft, creamy dish.

"It's how my grandmother taught me," Daniela says, smiling as she shares this memory. And so each of us slips into a long line of Italian tradition—learning the secrets behind the country's delicious dishes, thanks to the abundant, generous spirit of its cooks.

TOURS

Daniela del Balzo Cooking In Rome: www.contexttravel.com

12 *Study Italian in Rome*

"GET AN ITALIAN BOYFRIEND," is what girlfriends tell me is the best way to learn the language. Learning to speak Italian while falling in love is a lot like how a baby makes its first attempts. First it's all about *amore*, then it moves on to basic necessities where you're like a demanding two-year-old, and if things go further, you'll inevitably be expressing feelings, which could lead to anything from a tearful breakup or, in the case of my friend Lisa, a happy marriage and two adorable bilingual children.

Going another route, you could sign yourself up for language school. It's a great way to immerse yourself in the culture, and if you're traveling alone, there's a built-in social scene.

Rome is full of good schools. Years ago, I enrolled in **Ciao Italia**, a small place near the Colosseum, that my Italofile friend Louise had recommended. They fixed me up with budget accommodations (my own bedroom and bath) in a huge Trastevere apartment, where I was hosted by Antoinella, a half-deaf, seventy-something widow. She insisted on feeding me, and I got a kick out of hanging out and watching blaring TV with her just like I'd done back in Jersey with my *nana*.

My classmates were a writer from Edinburgh who was working on translating Belli (his favorite Roman poet), a thirty-something Venezuelan gal who'd married an Italian and was on a job hunt, and a Japanese chef who worked in an Italian restaurant in Tokyo. It's a typical mix—most of the time you won't find many Americans in these schools.

The instructors were enthusiastic types, who rode Vespas to work and looked like fashionistas even when they were just wearing jeans and zip-up jackets. The classes were excellent and structured as most of the language schools in Italy are: three-hour morning sessions, broken up into grammar and conversation classes, and optional afternoon activities that ranged from cooking classes to a walking tour of the Jewish Ghetto, or watching *Cinema Paradiso* without subtitles. Teaching was the "direct method," with classes totally in Italian. It was rigorous, with homework, but all added up to two intense weeks of a lot of fun.

The best part was the speedy learning curve. All of a sudden I was in the living room with my Trastevere *nonna* who was telling me a convoluted story about the chicken she had bought that morning, and how it reminded her of her late husband who hated chicken, maybe because her mother always made chicken when she lived with them when they first married...and I realized...Eureka!...Ho Capito!...I understand!

Ciao Italia: Check out the website for the range of programs they offer, along with accommodation arrangements, at great prices: www.ciao-italia.it.

OTHER LANGUAGE SCHOOLS IN ROME

Divulgazione Lingua Italiana: www.dilit.it

Scuola Leonardo da Vinci: www.scuolaleonardo.it

13 *Hiking and Biking in Rome*

The Roman Walk

A beautiful way to start a Roman day is to take a walk up to the Janiculum Hill. You leave the historic center, cross the Ponte Sisto, wander the streets of Trastevere, and then head up Via Garibaldi. Things quiet down as the via curves, and the panorama of Rome begins to emerge in the distance...dome after dome...and then—*ta-da!*—you come face to face with the magnificent *Fontana dell'Acqua Paola* (aka *Fontanone*, Big Fountain), an enormous Baroque stunner from the seventeenth century, built using white marble from the ruins of the Temple of Minerva. This was the inspiration for the Trevi Fountain, and I've often seen brides and grooms posing here for photos.

Continue to the hilltop, where on weekend mornings there are often puppet shows, with a rapt audience of *bambini*, clapping and shouting at the comical characters playing out classical stories in the slapped-up-telephone-booth-sized stage.

While you're up there, don't miss the statue of **Anita Garibaldi**, Italy's wonder woman, who fought alongside her husband Giuseppe in the nineteenth-century revolution that culminated in giving them the titles "Father and Mother of Modern Italy." The statue captures Anita in a courageous pose, riding a wild mustang, brandishing a pistol in one hand, with a baby tucked under her other arm.

Anita's life story (partly told in the frieze below the statue) is the stuff of a blockbuster movie. She was born in Brazil and  learned horsemanship from her father, who died when she was twelve. At fourteen, she was married off to a local older man, Signor Aguiar, aka "the drunken shoemaker."

While her husband was off at war, Giuseppe Garibaldi sailed in from Italy, with a passion to help Brazil fight for its independence. The moment he set eyes on dark-haired Anita with her extraordinary almond-shaped eyes, Giuseppe walked straight up to her and proclaimed, "Maiden, thou shalt be mine." Even though she was still married, Anita dashed off to fight by Giuseppe's side in Brazil and Uruguay, firing cannons, teaching him gaucho guerrilla warfare, and giving birth to their first son in the midst of all that. They married two years later, after Anita's first husband died.

In 1848, with four children in tow (between the ages of eight and two!), Anita and Giuseppe left South America to go to Italy and join the fight for unification. A year later, Anita died in Giuseppe's arms after a battle near Ravenna. She was twenty-eight and pregnant with their fifth child.

Giuseppe (whose statue is also at the top of the hill) kept Anita's memory alive. When he rode in victory to the crowning of Emmanuel II, the first king of a united Italy, he wore a Brazilian poncho. And around his neck, Anita's striped scarf.

Biking in the Borghese Gardens

Rome's elegant park is 65 acres of manicured green, shadowed by umbrella pines, with wide flat paths that are perfect for leisurely biking. In the **Porto Pinciana** area, you can rent bikes or surrey-style pedal carts, and take off gliding around blooming gardens, magnolia trees, fountains, and the pond with its mini-Tempio di Esculapio.

Rent at *Bici Pincio* (two locations: Viale della Pineta, Viale di Villa Medici; four euros an hour)

Biking the Appian Way

On a weekday afternoon, when tourists are few, and the light is soft and hazy, it's heavenly to bike along the Appian Way, nicknamed *Regina Viarum*, Queen of the Roads. The engineering triumph of this road began in 312 B.C., connecting Rome with Brindisi. In 1988, this section—from the center of Rome to the Alban Hills—was turned into a regional park. Basalt stones of the original road, where chariots traveled, still remain along many stretches, flanked by grassy fields, catacombs, tombs, and crumbling statues.

My ideal ride begins past the entrance and catacombs, near the park's largest tomb, from 50 B.C., dedicated to **Cecilia Metella**, who was the daughter-in-law of a mega-rich Roman. The tomb was turned into a fortress in the fourteenth century, which is why you'll see the crenellated walls at the top.

Riding can be bumpy along the stones, but there are smoother dirt paths cut into the bordering grass, and you can turn off the main road to wind around paved lanes and catch glimpses of grand villas behind ivy-covered gates. Bird songs and stately cypress trees surround you, and then...you may hear the tinkling of bells and look over a stone wall to discover a herd of goats grazing in an open field.

Parco Appia Antica: www.parcoappiaantica.it

꙳ᴗ

Golden Day: Taxi or bus (#118) to the Tomb of Cecilia Metella and rent a bike nearby for a couple of blissful hours. Eat at **Hostaria Antica Roma**, (Via Appia Antica, 87, 06 513 2888, closed Monday, www.anticaroma.it) that's set in a building from Imperial Days, which was once a mausoleum for freed slaves. These days, thanks to the Magnanimi family, who found it abandoned and restored/renovated it in the 1980s, it's the perfect place to prolong the step-back-in-time atmosphere, and enjoy delicious Roman classics.

TIP: *Bike rental: Appia Antica Caffè, www.appiaanticacaffe.it, open 10-sunset, a two-minute walk from the Tomb of Cecilia. This is a better choice than the Tourist Information bike rental, where the park begins. Farther in, at the Tomb of Cecilia, you can take off to the area that's less crowded with catacomb visitors.*

14 *Roman Spas & Hair Salons*

FROM THE EARLY DAYS OF THE EMPIRE, Romans reveled in the pleasures of spas and beauty treatments. The tradition continues...

Wellness Zone at Hotel de Russie

The perfect stop for my Italy arrival day is this glamorous spa, an oasis done up in creamy white, orchids, and candles scenting rooms with an enticing spicy aroma. It's downstairs from the chic Hotel de Russie, located between the Spanish Steps and Piazza Popolo, and backed by the Borghese Gardens. The expert staff of warm, welcoming *signoras* customizes jet-lag treatments— mine included an ayurvedic massage, dip in the hydropool, and Turkish bath. They also offer a Roman Foot Ritual, (soothing for after sightseeing), as well as a full range of body treatments, facials, and hair styling.

Relax afterwards in the hotel's Secret Garden, a popular afternoon tea and aperitivo spot for Romans. And don't miss the lobby's **Farella** boutique, which carries a luxurious line of lighter than air cashmere and silk scarves, handmade by four artisan sisters from Capri.

Hotel de Russie: Via del Babuino 9, 06 32 88 8820, open daily 7-10 (www.hotelderussie.it)

Spazio Beauty, Via dei Chiavari 37, 06 686 9800
A simple "Beauty Place" off the Campo dei Fiori, where you can get massages, body scrubs, facials, and waxing for reasonable prices.

Contesta Rock Hair, Via degli Zingari 9, 06 478 23717, closed Sunday and Monday (www.contestarockhair.com)
In the Monti neighborhood, near the Colosseum, this modern shop is not just for rock and rollers as the name might imply. It's a great place to get a chic, reasonably priced cut and then stop next door at their boutique to buy some hip clothes to match.

Shopping in Rome

THE MOST GLAMOROUS ROME SHOPPING can be found around the **Spanish Steps,** with the pedestrian only **Via Condotti** at its center, flanked by Italy's superstars of the fashion world, including **Ferragamo, Gucci, Tod's,** and **Max Mara.**

To the left of the steps, is **Furla** (Piazza di Spagna 22), a wonderland for purse seekers. And Via Condotti ends with **Palazzo Fendi** (Largo Goldoni), a shrine to leather and fur. The **Fendi** empire all began with a talented, determined woman: Adele Casagrande, who created a little fur shop in 1918, then married, and encouraged her five daughters to join the business that's become a sensational success worldwide. Loyal to Rome, the company's latest project is to restore Rome's fountains, including the **Fountain of Trevi.**

For **vintage and boutique shops,** around the corner from **Piazza Navona,** stroll down **Via del Governo Veccchio,** where highlights include:

* **Maga Morgana,** Via del Governo Vecchio 27 and 98
  These two shops, run by designer Luciana Lannace, carry a range from vintage t-shirts to gorgeous dresses and splendid bridal wear.

● **Tempi Moderni**, Via del Governo Vecchio 108
This is a fun stop to hunt around for costume jewelry and accessories from the 1920s to the 1950s.

Here are some favorite shops in the Historic Center for...

Leather

● **Ibiz,** Via dei Chiavari 39 (near Campo dei Fiori)
Elisa Nepi, a young Roman artisan, is the designer of every chic thing in this fun shop. She also (bless her) keeps her prices for handcrafted wallets, purses, and belts reasonable. Her parents started the business in 1972, making satchels for local workmen that became popular with backpackers. In 2002, Elisa was all set to fly the coop and become a physical therapist. But when she flunked her university exam, she decided to put her hands into the business and has brought the shop into the fashion limelight.

● **Sirni**, Via della Stelletta 33 (near Campo Marzio, www.sirnipelletteria.it)
The Sirni family has been in the Rome leather business for over a hundred years. Come to this sophisticated, tiny shop for exquisitely handcrafted luxury bags, some done up in crocodile or ostrich leather. Roman women adore Sirni for their customized services; you can have them make a purse for you with every compartment you'd ever desire. It'll take a month, since it's a small workshop, but to have something beautifully styled by these folks is worth the wait.

Shoes

⚜ **Dal Co'**, Via Vittoria 65 (near Spanish Steps, www.dalco-roma.com)
Gina Lollobrigida and Ava Gardner were fans of this exclusive shop that custom makes to-die-for women's shoes.

Lingerie

⚜ **Brighenti**, Via Frattina 7 (near Piazza di Spagna, www.brighentiboutique.it)
This is the prettiest lingerie shop I've ever seen. Crystal chandeliers hang over two floors of elegant rooms, displaying layers of delicate lace bras and panties. You'll sigh over racks of gelato-colored silk negligees, and matching jewel-ornamented mules. The dressing rooms, frescoed in pale turquoise and gold, entice you to try something on, and the prices are surprisingly not astronomic.

Jewelry

⚜ **Studio Gioielleria R. Quattrocolo**, Via della Scrofa 48 (near Campo Marzio, www.quattrocolo.com)
This antique jewelry shop has enticing displays of gold, coral, cameos, and gems. Most unique are the micro-mosaic pieces, created to replicate souvenirs from the days of the Grand Tour, with scenes of ancient ruins, mythological figures and landscapes.

❀ **Diego Percossi Papi**, Via Sant'Eustachio 16 (near the Pantheon, www.percossipapi.com)
Sophia Loren and Naomi Campbell are fans of Percossi's shimmering, colorful creations. He uses a unique cloisonné enamel technique, incorporating precious and semi-precious gems and pearls into his beautiful designs.

❀ **Filippo Moroni**, Via Belsiana 32A (near the Spanish Steps)
Since Rome's *La Dolce Vita* party days, Moroni has been creating bold, dramatic jewelry, using coral, semi-precious and precious gems.

Perfume, Soaps, etc.

❀ **Ai Monasteri,** Corso del Rinascimento 72 (near Piazza Navona, www.emonasteri.it)
A simple two-room spot, attractively stocked with varieties of monk-made beauty products, along with chocolates, honey, liqueurs, and marmalades made in abbeys all over Italy. It's been around since 1864 and is still run by the Nardi family, who started it all when they teamed up with the Benedictine Order of hard-working monks.

Favorites are Antica Acqua di Colonia perfume, a bergamot-and-musk blend created for the 1900 World Exhibition, and soap scented with violets of Parma. Everything is beautifully packaged and reasonably priced, making this a great spot for girlfriend gifts.

Antique Market

* **Ponte Milvio Antique Market**, first Sunday of the month
  (near Piazza Mancini)

The neighborhood surrounding Rome's oldest bridge is one of the city's hippest. Historically, it's where Emperor Constantine won the battle that began the Christian era in 312 a.d. The market here sells a range of antique and vintage items, as well as handcrafts. It's a far better option than the Porta Portese market in Trastevere, which gets schlockier every year.

Books

* **Almost Corner Bookshop**, Via del Moro 45, Trastevere
  A great selection of quality books (in English) fill this delightful shop, run by ex-pat Irishman Dermot and a lovely, helpful crew.

❧

Golden Day: Have your fun on Via Condotti and then lunch at **Ristorante Museo Canova Tadolini**, in the space that once was the atelier of the famous sculptor, Canova. It's now stuffed with his dramatic statues. A plus to this choice is that it serves from noon to 11 P.M. without a break, also a good stop for caffè. (Via del Babuino, 150/a, www.canovatadolini.com)

TOURS

For Guided Shopping Tours of Rome: www.grandtourshopping.com

16 Live Music, Opera, and Puppet Shows in Rome

ROME HAS LOTS OF LIVE blockbuster entertainment events, such as summer **Opera at the Baths of Caracalla** (www.operaroma. it), and performances of the **Accademia Nazionale di Santa Cecilia** (Rome's Symphony Orchestra and Chorus—named in honor of the Trastevere saint) at the **Auditorium Parco delle Musica of Roma** (www.auditorium.com), a marvelous modern theater complex, designed by superstar architect Renzo Piano. Check their schedules before your visit to buy tickets in advance.

Or maybe an evening's entertainment will happen more spontaneously. In the historic center, you'll often walk by posters announcing a classical chamber music concert in a church, and you can slip in for a lovely musical overture to dinner. One of my favorite spots:

❀ **Sacristy of Borromini–Piazza Navona**
  Right off Piazza Navona, in the back of the **Church of Saint Agnes in Agony,** is this jewel box venue, designed by the Baroque master Borromini. Guest artists—from award-winning young players to musicians of international fame—bring in a varied repertoire, so your program may include Schubert, Paganini, Debussy, Mozart, Brahms, Liszt, or Chopin. Concerts usually start around 6 P.M. and run about an hour or so.

Tickets: 335 608 1277, www.santagneseinagone.org

Also, **Concerti del Tempietto** is a cultural organization that hosts classical music concerts in churches and historical venues in Rome, including the **Theatre of Marcellus**, in the summer. Tickets are free or low cost. (www.tempietto.it)

For Jazz, Roman style

* **Gregory Jazz Club**

  A cozy spot near the Spanish Steps that hosts top-of-the-line players, offering dinner downstairs and a whisky tasting bar with over 100 varieties. (Via Gregoriana 54/a, 06 679 6386, closed Monday, dinner reservations essential, shows start around 10 P.M., www.gregorysjazz.com)

* **Casa del Jazz**

  Praised as one of the best jazz venues in Europe, this former villa of a Roman criminal boss was confiscated by the government and turned into a jazz cultural center that opened in 2005, with a theater, library, restaurant, and outdoor performance spaces. The weekend brunch is a blast. (Viale di Porta Ardeatina 55, 06 704 731, www.casajazz.it)

Puppet Shows—Fun for the Whole Family

* **Teatrino di Pulcinella al Gianicolo**

  Puppet shows have been performed on the Gianiculum Hill for decades, a tradition beloved by generations of Romans. The stage is telephone-booth sized, and the action-packed stories star the Neapolitan clown, *Pulcinella*. He's the big-nosed rascal in the baggy white pants, who is always causing trouble. Typically, he's after the buxom servant, Colombina,

who cleverly saves the day. Full of slapstick that keeps the enraptured audience of *bambini* and their parents clapping, shouting, and laughing. (Gianiculum Hill, behind Garibaldi's statue, Monday-Sunday at 4 and 7 P.M., Saturday and Sunday at 10:30 A.M., 1 P.M., 4 P.M., 7 P.M., though times may vary. Shows run about 1/2 hour. Free—a hat is passed at the end.)

* **San Carlino**
This charming, 100-seat theatre in the Borghese Gardens presents traditional *Pulcinella* puppet shows, along with fairytales, such as *Little Red Riding Hood* and *Pinocchio*. A great stop for families, with lots more in the surrounding park to make for a perfect day of play: pond with paddleboats, merry-go-round, mini diesel train, and *bioparco* (zoo). (Viale dei Bambini in Borghese Gardens, Saturdays and Sundays, www.sancarlino.it)

Estate Romane: Every summer, Rome celebrates with a series of events throughout the city, many of them free, including outdoor film showings, dance, theatre, and music. (www.estateromana.comune.roma.it)

Rome Entertainment Listings:
www.inromenow.com, www.romeguide.it

Side Trips
from Rome

Villa d'Este, Tivoli

BEFORE YOU EVEN GET TO THIS GARDEN, you hear rushing water. Then you stand above majestic terraces filled with countless sculpted fountains, ponds, and grottoes. Water shoots up in grand columns, arcs out of a hundred animal heads, tumbles like a curtain over caves, pumps through a stone organ that plays a classical tune. On and on and on, it's High Renaissance Aqua-Theater.

Villa d'Este was Cardinal Ippolito II d'Este's spectacular reaction to getting a booby prize. In the mid-sixteenth century, he lost out on becoming pope. The powers that were in Rome shooed him away to suburban Tivoli and gave him the job of governor. Instead of living a life of luxury in the papal apartments, he was exiled to government housing: a plain ol' former Benedictine convent.

Being the rich Renaissance guy that he was, Ippolito embraced the "Man Controls Nature" philosophy of his day. Reaching back to the glory of ancient Rome, he built a massive aqueduct, diverting the plentiful waters of the Aniene River to his back yard. He pillaged the nearby Villa of Hadrian, using the former Emperor's marble and statues to make his home magnificent. He threw elaborate banquets, stocking his ponds with fish for his guests to catch and then hand over to servants to cook up. Folks came and marveled over the waterworks, calling it d'Este's "Garden of Miracles." *Living Well Is the Best Revenge* became his mantra.

Ippolito could have sulked and blamed his late *mamma*, Lucrezia Borgia, for his dreary Tivoli assignment. Lucrezia's father, Pope Alexander VI, had headed up a family of notorious Borgia villains who'd run the Vatican's reputation into the dirt. Lucrezia was the beauty of the clan, rumored to have worn a hollow ring filled with poison that she'd drip into cups of those the family found undesirable. Her first two husbands were gotten rid of by the Borgia men when they didn't cooperate with the family's evil plans.

The Duke of Ferrara (Alfonso d'Este) became Lucrezia's third husband and father to Ippolito. Their marriage had glimmers of respectability. Sure, Lucrezia had her affairs—with the popular poet Bembo and, most naughtily, with the husband of that paragon of virtue, Isabella d'Este. But the Duke played around too and pretty much let Lucrezia's dalliances slide. To the outside world, the couple put on a classy royalty show. Lucrezia bore seven children and became zealously religious in her later years, until she died in childbirth at thirty-nine. Still, her *femme fatale* legacy would never disappear, which mucked up Ippolito's chance at becoming pope.

Which is why at Tivoli he pumped up the fact that he was a d'Este, and downplayed his Borgia connection. His whole d'Este paternal line had glorified themselves by wackily tracing their roots back to Hercules, so Ippolito filled his home and garden with allusions to the hero.

He had a villa room frescoed with a triumphant scene of Hercules in the Garden of Hesperides. According to legend, the strong man was challenged to go to this garden and pick an immortality-inducing golden apple that grew on a tree guarded by three "nymphs of the night," called Hesperides. All over Villa d'Este there are frescos including lemons, and lush pots of them in the garden, symbolizing those golden apples.

You'd hardly know this place was owned by a cardinal, or that it was even a former convent, as it has a smorgasbord of pagan images. Goddesses make their appearances in Ippolito's bedroom—there's a wall fresco of the gadabout Venus, and to balance things out, a chaste Diana on the ceiling. Ippolito put another version of Diana, as nature goddess of Ephesus, spouting water from what appears to be multiple breasts (actually they symbolized sacrificial bull's testicles), smack in front of the water organ. But conservative types that came in 1611 moved that Diana to the more discreet corner you'll find it in today.

Minerva, Goddess of Wisdom and Rome, crowns the Rometta fountain, a mini-model of the Eternal City. It's at the top of the terraces, facing Rome. You can imagine Ippolito standing right there, amidst his happy guests—from cardinals to courtesans—as they romped about his playground. No doubt he'd take in the whole scene, look past Minerva towards the city that rejected him, and smile.

Villa d'Este: Tuesday-Sunday 8:30-one hour before sunset (www.villadestetivoli.info)

✤

Golden Day: Visit the **Villa d'Este** and the nearby **Hadrian's Villa.** It's best to go to the latter with a tour group, because like the Roman Forum, it's a huge, sprawling place and practically none of the ruins are marked. Eat at **Osteria La Briciola**, where you are graciously served seasonal specialties, beautifully prepared. Get a seat on the terrace to enjoy a great view. (Via Tiburtina Valeria 106, Tivoli, 0774 418421, reservations essential, closed Monday, open for dinner Tuesday-Sunday, lunch Saturday-Sunday only, www.osterialabriciola.it)

How to get there: The easiest way is by joining a group tour, as there are many to choose from that also include Hadrian's Villa, such as Context Travel (www.contexttravel.com). Or rent a car and drive twenty miles on the Rome-L'Aquila Autostrada, exiting at A24. You could also take a Cotral bus (www.cotralspa.it) that you can catch at Rome's Metro Linea B, Ponte Mammolo station. Allow an hour to get there.

RECOMMENDED READING

The Cardinal's Hat: Money, Ambition, and Everyday Life in the Court of a Borgia Prince by Mary Hollingsworth

18 Celebrate the Goddess Diana in Nemi

WHEN ANCIENT ROMANS GOT TO this lush, forested place, they discovered the Latin tribe before them had been worshipping a female goddess here. The Romans declared the place divine and built a Temple to Diana, Virgin Goddess of Fertility, the Moon, and the Hunt. They called the place Nemi, from the Latin, *Nemus*, Sacred Grove. They called the lake that bordered the forest the *Specchio di Diana* (Mirror of Diana), because it so finely reflected the moon above. Women came to the temple to pray for children and easy deliveries.

Today Nemi is known as the smallest and most enchanting village in the Castelli Romani, an area that lies fifteen miles south of Rome. Most of the *castelli*, castles, from medieval days are long gone, and what remains is a bucolic cluster of sixteen towns and villages, scattered through the gentle Alban Hills. The most famous of the bunch are **Frascati** (known for its wine), and **Castelo Gandolfo,** home to the pope's summer palace.

Long ago the hills were the sides of a volcano, so the land is fertile. Vineyards, orchards, and fields of vegetables and flowers thrive here. Adding beauty to the Castelli Romani are remnants of Roman villas and temples, medieval monasteries, grand churches and Renaissance palazzos.

In the Eternal City's imperial days, emperors fled up to these hills to escape the summer heat. The most insane of those emperors, Caligula, hell bent on aligning himself with the goddess Diana, had two fantastical ships built on Lake Nemi: one a floating temple to honor her, the other an opulent party boat with marble floors, stately columns, and intricate plumbing. During his short reign, Lake Nemi was The Place to Be for fabulous celebrations. Then Claudius took over as Emperor, and sank Caligula's ships. They remained protected under water and silt, stirring the imaginations of those who had read about the legendary vessels. Many made pilgrimages here to stare into the lake, hoping to get a glimpse of the ships.

Cut to Mussolini, on his own mad mission to align himself with imperial days, who took on the massive project of draining Lake Nemi to dredge up Caligula's ships. In 1932, onlookers stood by astounded as these incredible treasures from the ancient world, remarkably well preserved, were revealed to them. The Museo delle Navi Romane was built to display the newly discovered artifacts, and then, tragically, in 1944, the museum was burned by the Germans during a hasty retreat. Still, you can visit the museum and see what remains—including impressive bronze lion heads, a hull that has been rebuilt to show the grandeur of Caligula's days, and photos of the 1932 excavation. In the nearby forest you can discover ruins of Diana's temple—columns, mosaic floors, and wall paintings.

Travelers on the nineteenth-century Grand Tour reveled in Nemi's magical appeal. Turner painted the lake and Lord Byron sang its praises in his poem, *Childe Harold's Pilgrimage:*

> *Lo, Nemi! navell'd in the woody hills . . .*
> *The oval mirror of thy glassy lake; . . .*
> *All coil'd into itself and round, as sleeps the snake.*

To add to its allure, there's a sweet deliciousness. Nemi is famous for *fragoline di bosco*, wild strawberries, which grow in the forests surrounding the lake. All over the village, shops display abundant baskets of *fragoline* and every eatery—from bakeries to restaurants—offers *fragoline* specialties—from tarts, to cakes, gelato, and custards. If you're lucky to come the first weekend in June, you'll find a *Sagra delle Fragoline*, festival, with lovely *signorinas* in costume dancing about, giving free *fragoline* to all—as graceful and fun loving as the goddess Diana herself.

Museo delle Navi Romane, Via del Tempio di Diana 13, open Monday-Saturday, 9-7, Sunday 9-1 (www.museonaviromane.it)

In Italy Tours, www.initalytours.com, offers excellent customized tours of the Castelli Romani, including cooking classes, visits to artisans, wineries, and sketching classes if desired.

❧

Golden Day: Stroll through Nemi, stopping at the **Bar Panoramico** to admire the dreamy view of the lake below, as you enjoy your *fragoline* treat—I'm partial to a few *fragoline* dropped into a flute of prosecco to set the mood, though others may prefer the frozen fragoline daiquiri. Take a drive down to the **Museo delle Navi Romane** and wander in the forest to see the ruins of Diana's Temple. Continue on to explore more places in the Castelli Romani at your leisure.

Shopping

You have your choice of *fragoline*-themed souvenirs—including liqueurs and marmalades. There are also some cute handicraft shops, including **Sogni nelle Mani**, where Signora Maria Di Benedetto makes lace, and even holds lacemaking classes upon request. (Corso Vittorio Emanuele 21, 06 937 5759)

Eating in the Castelli

The traditional Castelli Romani lunch takes place in the town of **Ariccia**, home to *fraschette*—casual eateries that in days past were places where the new wine was tasted and customers brought in their own food. These days *fraschette* specialize in *porchetta* (roasted spiced pork), and many places serve tasting platters of cured meats and cheeses. You'll find a bunch of rowdy *fraschette* with outdoor tables along **Via Borgo San Rocco**, where, if you order simply (just antipasti), you'll be okay and can eat a lot for a bargain. Or, for a better lunch, in the central piazza, go to **Ariccia De Mi Zia**, that serves a low-priced two-course meal—antipasti, pasta, and drinks included. (Via Corso Garibaldi 6, 347 439 6147, reservations a must, www.fraschette-ariccia.it)

For a very special meal, head to **Osteria di San Cesario** Celebrity Chef Anna Dente, internationally praised as *The Queen of Amatriciana*, reigns here, deliciously preserving the tradition of authentic Roman cuisine. (Via F. Corridoni 60, San Cesareo, 06 958 7950, closed Monday, www.annadente.it)

TIP: *If you come in the warmer months, you can bathe in Lake Nemi, considered sacred waters by the ancients. Have a local show you the best route to get to the bathing spot, as much of the lakeside is private residences.*

19 Sperlonga

"A ROMAN SUMMER ISN'T A REAL Roman summer without a stay in **Sperlonga**," says my friend Gioia, an Eternal City native. She's been going there every August for twenty years. "It's where we all had our first boyfriends," she sighs.

Set high up on a seaside cliff, Sperlonga's historic center has the ambiance of an old Greek city: a pedestrian-only labyrinth of whitewashed stone buildings connected by stairways and arched alleys. Though now it's basically a tourist town, Sperlonga retains the quaint atmosphere of its fishing village days—pre-1957, before a road was built to reach this place. It's always attracted liberal, creative types like the Italian writer Natalie Ginzburg who had a home here. And because it's positioned halfway between Rome and Naples, it's a popular spot with visitors from both cities.

Stretching out below the town are immaculately raked beaches of golden sand and the tantalizing, rolling, cobalt sea. Modern beach establishments cover the area north of Sperlonga harbor, but to the south is where you'll find the treasures of free beaches and classic clubs, where rentals of umbrellas and chairs are about twenty euros. Gioia's advice is to head to Lido Grotta dei Delfini. "It's one of the quieter beaches, with beautiful wide white umbrellas, and room to spread out and enjoy everything."

In the evenings, the Sperlonga *piazzetta* is a charming place to relax with a cocktail and enjoy a sunset view. And in traditional Italian beach-town fashion, outdoor movies are shown—a different one every night to entertain the whole family.

For a break from the sun, walking south along the shore takes you to the **Museo Archeologico di Sperlonga**—ruins of a Roman villa, cave, and museum. Here's where the Emperor Tiberius, who reigned from A.D. 14 to A.D. 37, would come to party, before he moved permanently to Capri. The cave had an island inside it that was his banquet room, and submerged in the surrounding waters were sculptures that told stories from Homer's *Odyssey*. You can see in the museum these enormous statues of such dramatic scenes as the multi-headed Scylla she-monster eating up Odysseus's crew or the blinding of the Cyclops Polyphemus.

Museo Archeologico di Sperlonga: www.sperlonga.IT.it

❧

Golden Day: Get to **Lido Grotta dei Delfini** (www.grottadeidelfini.it, entrance fee of 20 to 30 euros includes umbrellas and beach beds). Enjoy a seafood dinner with a view at **Tramonto Bistrot** (Corso San Leone 21, 0771 549597). Stay in the historic center at **Hotel Corallo** (www.corallohotel.com), a cozy three-star.

How to get there: It's best to drive, which takes about two hours from Rome. Or take a train from Roma Termini to the Fondi-Sperlonga stop, and then connect to Sperlonga by bus or taxi.

TIP: *Best months to visit are May and October. Avoid weekends in July and August, when it's mobbed with Italian vacationers.*

II

Florence

"When I arrived in Florence for the first time, I felt that it was familiar, that I had felt Florence before. It has a seductive spell. I feel part of the eternal, whilst at the same, living in the moment. Not surprisingly, in this place of paradoxes."
—FREYA MIDDLETON, FLORENCE TOUR GUIDE

In 60 B.C., when Roman soldiers found this spot, they named it "Florentia," meaning "may *she* flourish." Over thousands of years Florence has become a center of revival, the *Cradle of the Renaissance*, where artworks celebrate feminine curves of goddesses and the Annunciation of the Madonna—that transformational moment where a woman is told: *The Divine Is Within You!* In fact, the Feast of the Annunciation, on March 25, was when Florentines traditionally celebrated their New Year, and to this day festivities take place here on that date.

At the center of it all is the dazzling Duomo, aka **Basilica di Santa Maria del Fiore**, a triumph of the Renaissance. The Humanist philosophers of those days believed that the worship of beauty was key to connecting to the divine spirit. You'll have plenty of opportunities to do just that, entering churches and museums, as if you're opening one jewelry box after another.

Take your time to wander through the Oltrarno, on the artsy side of the river, linger in a caffè to admire beautiful

Florentines, whose faces resemble the characters you'll see in the city's paintings. There is inspiration at every turn.

Along with my suggestions, major attractions:

Piazza del Duomo, with Duomo, Baptistry of San Giovanni, Ghiberti's Doors of Paradise, Giotto's Campanille, Museo dell'Opera: In the Museo dell'Opera, don't miss *Michelangelo's Deposition (aka Florence Pieta)* and Donatello's *Penitent Magdalene.* www.ilgrandmuseodelduomo.it

Gallerie dell'Accademia, Michelangelo's *David:* He's more amazing in person than in his photographs. Be sure to reserve a ticket to avoid the lines. www.uffizi.firenze.it

Museo Nazionale del Bargello: Extraordinary sculptures here, including Donatello's **David** and Bernini's bust of **Costanza Bonarelli.** www.polomuseale.firenze.it

RECOMMENDED READING

Brunelleschi's Dome: How a Renaissance Genius Reinvented Architecture by Ross King

20 Venuses, Madonnas, and Judith at the Uffizi

RENAISSANCE PAINTERS OF FLORENCE created loads of masterpieces that glorified females. In the city's major museum, the **Uffizi**, you'll see women adored in such paintings as those that follow.

The Birth of Venus, 1484, by Sandro Botticelli (Rooms 10-14)

Describing a woman as a Botticelli automatically brings up this famous image of a naked, curvy Venus stepping off a seashell to

the shore. But Botticelli actually translates to "little barrel." It was the artist's nickname, because in truth he was a roly-poly guy.

A better description of a beautiful woman would be to call her a "Simonetta Vespucci," the name of the model for this painting. Simonetta was Botticelli's muse, the most adored woman in Florence, and his neighbor's wife.

She came to Florence from Genoa as the fifteen-year-old bride of Marco Vespucci, whose cousin was the famous Italian explorer Amerigo. Her fans called her *La Bella Simonetta* and liked to say she was born in the Ligurian coastal town of Portovenere, where the Romans believed Venus arose from the sea.

Though these days she'd be ordered to do Pilates to tighten her abs, in 1469 Simonetta's pear shape was ideal. Only poor starving gals were skinny back then, and Renaissance guys adored chicks with childbearing hips. In Florence, artists clamored to have Simonetta pose for them, writers sent her love poems, and she was showered with gifts from admirers.

The brothers Lorenzo and Giuliano de Medici, the family who ran Florence at the time, introduced Simonetta to Botticelli, an artist on the rise. Lorenzo, who was involved with being Magnificent and his banking and philosophy biz, ordered a painting of Simonetta for his bed chamber, which some say became Botticelli's *Venus*.

Giuliano, a sporty type, starred in a jousting tournament to be held in honor of this glamour-puss who had quickly become the Marilyn Monroe of Florence. Botticelli painted Giuliano's joust banner with the words "The Unparalleled One" under Simonetta's image. Giuliano won and Simonetta was declared "Queen of Beauty." Since she was married, there's no record of nooky between Simonetta and Giuliano, though the locals imagined their steamy affair as fervently as the Brangelina romance of our times.

A year after the joust, twenty-two-year-old Simonetta died of consumption. Her funeral was an Italian day of mourning. Thousands came to Florence to join in her casket procession, weeping and tossing flowers.

Botticelli had started painting *The Birth of Venus* before Simonetta died. It took him nine years to finish it, perhaps because the thought of his muse being gone from him was too tragic to bear.

As you look around the room, you'll see how Botticelli used Simonetta's inspiration again and again—from *Primavera* to *The*

Annunciation. He never married, in fact said the idea of marriage was a nightmare. And there were reports of him "liking boys," followed by charges of sodomy, that were dropped.

When he died, thirty-four years after *La Bella Simonetta*, Botticelli asked to be buried at her feet. In the Church of Ognissanti, which was Simonetta's family parish, you can see his wish was granted.

Venus of Urbino, 1538, by Titian (Room 28)

Here's the most erotic painting in the museum. Titian probably used a Venetian prostitute for his model, as there were around ten thousand in Venice during the time he did this painting, and they traditionally took on the extra work.

Venus stretches out on a couch *au naturale* in elegant surroundings, with a confident look and roses in one hand, that symbolize Venus. The most attention goes to her other hand, with her curled fingers between her legs.

The painting was commissioned by the Duke of Urbino, probably as a hint for his young bride. They married when the girl was only ten years old, but things couldn't be consummated—which meant the Duke couldn't have heirs—until she became a woman at fourteen. The medical belief in those days was that conception could only occur if both man and woman had orgasms, so Titian's Venus is teaching the Duke's bride how to do her wifely duty.

Madonna with Child and Two Angels, 1505-1506, by Filippo Lippi (Room 8)

In this totally enchanting painting, the Friar Lippi probably used the novice Lucrezia Buti as his model. The two had a scandalous love affair that led to her getting pregnant. The baby angel who is looking out from the painting is believed to be their child, who grew up to be the painter Filippino Lippi.

Annunciation, 1472-1475, by Leonardo da Vinci (Room 15)

It's amazing to think of Leonardo painting this when he was only twenty-one. Here Mary gracefully accepts her calling, looking up from her book, while the angel holds out a lily, the symbol of Florence.

Holy Family, aka Doni Tondo, 1506-1508, by Michelangelo (Room 25)

The master who sculpted the *David* and *Pieta* always claimed he wasn't good at painting, even though he painted the Sistine Chapel ceiling. He shows his genius here with vibrant color and signature sculptural sense of dimension. I see it as a great example of shared parenting, with Mary passing her son off to father Joseph, who seems to be able to handle it.

It was commissioned by the Doni family when their second child was born, as their first child had died in infancy. At first the Donis didn't appreciate Michelangelo's background nudes, but then accepted them as symbolic of the passing of pagan times.

Madonna of the Goldfinch, 1505, by Raphael (Room 26)

Mary, who symbolizes "The Seat of Wisdom," gets interrupted from reading by her son and his cousin, John the Baptist, at her feet. (It's my sister's favorite—as the mother of two she relates.) The goldfinch John the Baptist hands to Jesus is a symbol of his future violent death.

It was a wedding gift to Raphael's friend, was destroyed in an earthquake, breaking into seventeen pieces, and has undergone many meticulous restorations.

Judith Beheading Holofernes, 1614-1620, ### *by Artemisia Gentileschi (Room 43)*

Finally a painting by a woman! It's displayed on the lower floors along with some awesome Caravaggios, and was done by the great Renaissance artist Artemisia Gentileschi.

Gentileschi began painting in her father's workshop, showing her talent early on. She was raped by a painter her father teamed her up with, one Agostino Tassi. To ensure she was telling the truth during the trial where she accused Tassi, she was tortured. Horribly tortured, with a gynecological examination and wrapping and tightening of leather thongs around her fingers to the point of excruciating pain. It was believed if she could tell the same horrendous rape story under torture as the one she'd told as an accusation, it had to be true. Paintings such as this one, which tells the story of the Jewish heroine Judith cutting off the head of an enemy's general, have been interpreted as Gentileschi's revenge against that gruesome treatment.

Gentileschi's life story is ultimately inspiring. She went on to have a successful career and six children and was highly respected by her contemporaries, even though it was very unusual for a woman to be among them. Since she was passed over for the high altar commissions the men around her were getting, she moved around to find work—from Florence to Rome to Venice, and finally settled in Naples.

Feminists have always taken an interest in her life, and playwright Wendy Wasserstein used her in *The Heidi Chronicles*, in scenes of the main character lecturing about female painters.

Uffizi: open 8:15-6:50, 055 294 883, closed Monday (www.firenzemusei.it)

❧

Golden Day: Visit the **Uffizi**, then have dinner at **La Sostanza**, my favorite restaurant in Florence. It's a classic trattoria, always lively and delicious. Great to start with their *tortino di carciofi* (artichoke flan), followed by their amazing *bistecca* or chicken cooked in butter. Be sure to leave room for the meringue cake dessert. (Via Porcellana 25R, 055 212 691, reservations essential, closed Saturday and Sunday)

THREE TIPS: *(1) Be sure to make a reservation for the Uffizi Gallery to avoid long lines, either online, www.firenzemusei.it, or by phone, 055 294 883. (2) Afternoons are less crowded. (3) They only check-in backpacks and umbrellas, so if you have shopping bags, leave them at your hotel, so you don't have to tote them around the museum.*

RECOMMENDED READING

Invisible Women: Forgotten Artists of Florence by Jane Fortune, published by Advancing Women Artists Foundation. Check out www.advancingwomenartists.org for their events and projects in Florence.

Uffizi Art History Guide (App) by Alexander Korey of www.arttrav.com

21 Santa Maria Novella

ONE OF THE GREAT JOYS OF Italian travel is arriving by train to Florence, emerging from the *stazione*, and winding around to stand before the **Church of the New Saint Mary: Santa Maria Novella.** It's a dazzle of emerald and ivory marble, blending Gothic and Renaissance styles, dedicated to the Madonna of the Assumption, and packed with art inspired by the BVM.

This was the first great Florentine Basilica. Dominican friars, famous for their passionate preaching, began the project in 1279, to make room for their many followers. At the time, Florence was just a collection of humble huts, and Santa Maria Novella brought in a new architecture that the Dominican friars had seen while studyng in Bologna, Paris, and Cologne. The grandiose building kicked off the city's rise to glamorous fame and was further adorned in the fifteenth and sixteenth centuries.

Breakthrough art appears inside, which showcases the beginnings of the Renaissance. The most stunning examples are **Giotto's crucifix**, hanging in the center of the church, and on the left wall, **Masaccio's 3D *Trinity*** that astounded viewers with its masterful use of perspective.

Here are some female highlights:

Cappella Tornabuoni

Behind the central altar you'll discover this chapel, dedicated to the Madonna of the Assumption, covered with masterpiece frescoes by Renaissance artist **Ghirlandaio** and his workshop. Among his students was fourteen-year-old **Michelangelo**, who Ghirlandaio threw off the project when the young artist boldly began to redraw his designs.

Giovanni Tornabuoni, a big shot in the Medici banking world, commissioned this late fifteenth-century chapel. While today we associate Tornabuoni with the famous Via—Florence's fanciest shopping street—back then these frescoes are what shouted out the greatness of the Tornabuoni family. Giovanni probably chose Ghirlandaio for the job because the artist had a talent for portrait painting, and slipped in figures of family members throughout the biblical scenes. It's a great way to see how Florentines were dressing in those days (1486-1490), and Ghirlandaio's warm, clear style brings a deep humanity to every frame.

Focusing on the center of the chapel, in a lower panel, you'll see Giovanni kneeling, opposite his wife, **Francesca Pitti**, who died in childbirth in 1477.

The Life of the Virgin is told in the left fresco cycle. Starting at the bottom you'll see her birth, then presentation in the temple, annunciation, marriage, the birth of Christ, and her assumption into heaven. Curved above the window is her triumphant coronation.

On the right, the story continues with the **Life of John the Baptist**, aka **Giovanni the Baptist**, which donor Giovanni Tornabuouni probably also appreciated. Here you'll see the

Visitation, where Mary greets Elizabeth, who at an advanced age finds out she's pregnant with John the Baptist.

Focusing on Tornabuoni Ladies

* **Giovanna degli Albizi** can be seen in the Visitation, on the right, in sharp profile, wearing a golden brocade gown with her hair done up in a lovely braided-up do. She was from a noble family that held power before the Medici, and her beauty was legendary, not only in Florence, but all over Europe. She married Lorenzo Tornabuoni in an extravagant 1486 celebration, gave birth to a son, and then tragically in 1488, at the age of 20, died in childbirth with her second pregnancy. This portrait is a homage to her, and Ghirlandaio even included an inscription—a line from a Roman poet, that translates to: *Art, if only you could portray mores and spirit, there would be no more beautiful picture on earth.*

* **Dianora Tornabuoni,** the patron's sister, also appears in the Visitation, as the veiled woman dressed in black to the right of Giovanna, in the days when wives wore veils.

* **Lucrezia Tornabuoni**, another sister of Giovanni, appears in the Birth of John the Baptist—she's the older woman wearing blue shoes. Lucrezia was the wife of Piero de Medici, mother of Lorenzo the Magnificent—a noble, artsy woman who wrote sonnets.

* **Ludovica Tornabuoni,** Giovanni's only daughter, is painted in the fresco on the lower left: the Birth of Mary. Ludovica

stands in profile, with her hair in a long braid, wearing a dress similar to the beautiful Giovanna degli Albizi. Since Ludovica was only about 14 at the time of the painting, it must have been quite flattering to her (and her donor father) to be associated with the glamorous Giovanna.

The Tornabuoni chapel also honors the BVM with stained glass windows, designed by Ghirlandaio. One depicts the assumption, another the miraculous Madonna of the Snow, and another is of Mary giving her girdle (belt) to Saint Thomas—you can read more about that girdle in the Prato chapter.

Rucellai Chapel

On the right side of the main altar, you'll find this chapel dedicated to **Saint Catherine of Alexander**, the fourth-century martyr. She was a virgin beauty, devoted to Christ, who was condemned to death on a spiked wheel by the Emperor Maxentius. Miraculously, the wheel broke, so she was then beheaded. The painting is credited to Bugiardini, and many experts believe Michelangelo helped him out.

Tomb of Beata Villana

On the right side of the basilica, you'll find the elaborate marble tomb of an almost-saint from the fourteenth century. **Villana delle Botti** was born to a wealthy merchant family, but shunned all the riches, preferring fasting and hair shirts. Her parents were not on board with the piety behavior and married her off to a noble family. Surprisingly Villana didn't put up a fight, and blended into the world of elegance. That is until one day when she was all dolled up and took a look at herself in the mirror. To her horror, a demonic reflection appeared. She ordered her servants to bring another mirror, but the demon in the mirror persisted. When a third mirror brought the same result, Villana stripped off her gown, ran to Santa Maria Novella to confess her sins, put on a hair shirt and returned to a life of penitence and prayer, helping the poor. She went overboard with the fasting, died at 28, and was buried here. Her devoted grandson began a Villana cult, which attracted lots of followers, and in 1824 she was beatified.

Outside the basilica, other treasures glorifying females:

● **Cappella Della Pura**
This small chapel can be entered free from Via Avelli, through the Arch of the Faithful entrance. It's kept by the Dominicans as a beautiful spot for prayer, with a fourteenth-century fresco of the **Madonna and Child and St. Catherine.**

● **Spanish Chapel**
Don't miss the amazing fourteenth-century frescos in this chapel adjoining the Green Cloister, featuring jewel-toned images by Andrea di Boniauto, which illustrate the very complex philosophy of the Dominicans. It was renamed the Spanish Chapel in the sixteenth century, when it was given to Eleonora Toledo, who came from Spain to marry Cosimo de Medici and brought her Spanish entourage with her. (Read more about Eleonora in the Pitti Palace Costume Gallery chapter.)

Check out the women in the right wall fresco: *The Church Militant, Church Triumphant.* My eye is always drawn to those dancing beauties in the middle of it. According to the Dominicans, these women symbolize the perils of seductive pleasures—such as Lust, symbolized by the woman in the red dress with the monkey on her lap.

On the lower left there are four legendary women gathered to the side of the Duomo: Villana (in the black veil, whose story is told above) and stars of beloved poets: Dante's Beatrice, Boccaccio's Fiammetta, and Petrarch's Laura.

In the main altar fresco, the *Triumph of the Catholic Doctrine*, fourteen maidens are lined up on thrones, symbolizing good things, according to the Dominicans: the Sacred Sciences and the Liberal Arts—aspects of the intellect, which Dominicans believed should be perfected to reach God's salvation. There are stands with charts that will tell you all the characters and their meanings, but I believe you'd have to be a Dominican monk to absorb that all in one visit.

Santa Maria Novella: Piazza Santa Maria Novella, open Monday-Thursay 9-5:30, Friday 11-5:30, Saturday 9-5, Sunday (after morning mass) noon-5 (www.chiesasantamarianovella.it)

❧

Golden Day: Allow yourself an hour or more to visit the basilica and cloisters. Depending upon the time of day, you may want to head for a delicious Tuscan lunch at **Trattoria al Trebbio** (Via delle Belle Donne 47/49R, 055 287 089, closed Tuesday lunch). Or if you're more in the mood for a chic cocktail experience, slip into the **Hotel Brunelleschi's Tower Bar** (Piazza Sant'Elisabetta 3, 055 27370).

TIP: *There are two entrances to the complex: One from Piazza Santa Maria Novella and one from the Piazza della Stazione, just opposite the train station, next to the Tourist Information office. I've found the entrance from Piazza della Stazione to often be less crowded, and this is also the entrance that Florence Card holders must use.*

RECOMMENDED READING

Domenico Ghirlandaio: 95 Masterpieces by Maria Tsaneva

22 *Annunciations*

FLORENTINES ARE SO WILD ABOUT Mary they've always celebrated their New Year on her Annunciation, March 25. This is the day Catholics believe the Angel Gabriel swooped down to the Virgin Mary and said, *"The Divine is within you!"* telling her that she was pregnant with the Savior of the World.

These days there's partying to celebrate the event in the piazza of the **Church of the Most Holy Annunciation (Santissima Annunziata)**, where a thirteenth-century miracle is believed to have taken place. An artist (some say Pietro Cavallini) was painting a fresco of the Annunciation, and felt so overwhelmed when he got to the face, he stepped away and fell into a deep sleep. When he woke up, the painting was finished. (There's a universal dream of every artist if I've ever heard one.) The Annunciation fresco is to the left of the church entrance in an ornate tabernacle, and Florentine brides traditionally visit it to drop off their bouquets.

Besides the **Chiesa Santissima Annunziata**, Florence is chock-a-block with Annunciations. Renaissance painters loved interpreting the action-packed scene and the variations you'll see all over the city go from austere to absolutely flirty. I'm partial to Pontormo's Mannerist one in **Santa Felicitá**, where Mary's a willowy figure with a rose robe swirling about her, like a runway model.

The most famous Annunciation painting can be found in **Museo San Marco.** The Dominican Friars of this fifteenth-century monastery were very lucky to have a talented painter in their gang, Guido di Pietro. He was such a great guy, they named him Fra Angelico, which means Brother Angel. This Fra Angelico is not to be confused with the monk from northern Piedmont, for whom the hazelnut liqueur is named.

This Fra Angelico (now called Beato Angelico) spent eight years with his assistants frescoing San Marco's hallways and

monks' cells, with images to support them in their meditation and prayer. He was so spiritually on fire, he prayed every time he picked up a brush, never changed what he'd done (thinking it would insult the Divine who gave him inspiration), and wept every time he painted a crucifixion. The frescos here, painted over gold backgrounds downstairs and in muted jewel tones upstairs, clearly reflect his deep faith and humility.

On your way up the stairs to the cells, you'll turn on a landing and get hit with the sight of his most well-known Annunciation, which has been called the most beloved painting of the Renaissance. It's been reproduced so many times you'll get that weird brain readjustment that happens when suddenly you're in front of the real thing. Stay on that landing, with the stairs ahead of you to get the viewpoint Fra Angelico intended.

Peaceful power! Mary is timid, leaning forward with her hands crossed over her heart in acceptance. In its soft, luminous style, the moment of her transformation is striking. Taking in the whole image, you'll realize Fra Angelico's message. He included the beams of the house, to ground the event in reality.

At the same time the figures are totally out of proportion—as tall as the pillars and doors that surround them, so the expansive nature of the moment is palpable.

In Cell Number 3, believed to be Fra Angelico's, is a simpler Annunciation. There Saint Dominic, the monks' patron, stands in a corner. It's as if the painter, through the saint, was teaching the monks to contemplate this image of humility.

In 1982, Pope John Paul officially beatified Fra Angelico, praising the divine beauty he painted, and putting him on the path to become the Patron Saint of Artists.

Also in the Museo are beautiful paintings of Madonnas and female saints by other Fras. Two very memorable ones of the Virgin and Child by Fra Bartolomeo have been placed in one of the cells that belonged to Savonarola, the fanatic friar who inspired masterpieces to be burned in the famous 1497 Bonfire of the Vanities. Go figure.

Museo San Marco: Piazza San Marco, weekdays 8:15-1:50, weekends 8:15-4:15, closed first, third, and fifth Sundays, and second and fourth Mondays of the month (www.polomuseale.firenze.it)

❧

Golden Day: Visit **San Marco** in the morning, when the light is best for viewing the frescos. Then have lunch at **Trattoria Mario** (Via Rosina 2r, closed Sunday, no reservations), a great folksy place near the Mercato Centrale.

TIP: *Though the artwork here is amazing, this is a Florence museum that is not overcrowded.*

23 The Costume Gallery at the Pitti Palace

DUCHESS ELEONORA DI TOLEDO DE' MEDICI got fed up living in the gloomy Palazzo Vecchio. So in 1549, with her own money, she bought a palace on the other side of the Arno that the Pitti family had up for sale. What with her eight kids and failing health (hubby Duke Cosimo I had given her syphilis), Eleonora wanted someplace away from the city racket where she could have a garden. The choice was connected to her past: she'd been born in sunny Spain and grew up around lush gardens in Naples, the daughter of the city's Viceroy.

She was so raring to relocate she even moved in while renovations were going on, with architect Vasari doubling the palace in size. Right off the bat, she hired a landscaper for the backyard, which today we know as the Boboli Gardens.

Now the Pitti Palace Eleonora bought is home to six museums and those beautiful gardens. It's all too much for one visit, so I say go to the Costume Gallery for a change of scene from painting and sculpture. It's an absolutely glam place, the only museum in Italy dedicated to fashion design and is relatively new to the Pitti, opened in 1983.

You'll find it in the Palazzina della Meridiana, that was added to the palace and completed in 1858. Luscious chandeliers, gold-framed mirrors, and brocade walls decorate room after room (eighteen in all), that take you through 300 years of Italian fashion.

Displays rotate every two to three years, as the collection is vast. A memorable visit for me was an exhibit that began with eighteenth-century Marie Antoinette styles—impossibly wide skirts of richly textured fabrics. There were fantastic silk Neapolitan wedding dresses, satin bustled ensembles worn by contessas in the nineteenth century, beaded Italian flapper wear from the 1920s.

But what I most adored were the post-World War II fashions, where Italian designers broke loose and the styles were outrageously chic—from scrumptious 1950s cocktail dresses to sparkling gowns by Florentine designer Cesare Fabbri, and choice vintage pieces from revered fashion artists like Valentino, Gianfranco Ferre, and Maurizio Galante. It's fun to imagine Italian women out and about flaunting these threads. Many came from the closet of an eccentric Bologna department store heiress, Cecilia Matteucci Lavarini, who's world famous for collecting couture and has sent some of her overflow to the museum.

The last room of the exhibit honors Eleonora. The dress she was buried in is displayed there. It's in tatters, spread out in a glass case, but you still can get an idea of the style of this fabulous woman, who kept a staff of ten weavers working full time to create her elegant getups.

Eleonora married Cosimo I de' Medici in 1539, when she was seventeen and he was just a year older. The Medici rep was at a low point, so it was a coup for them to have this beautiful woman descended from Castilian royalty added to their mix.

Eleonora became a beloved first lady, winning the Florentines over with her generous patronage of artists and the peasantry. The marriage worked out: she put up with Cosimo's notorious mood swings, he put up with her penchant for gambling. He even named her regent when he'd take trips away from Florence, which was a most unusual position for a woman of those days.

Most importantly, Eleonora popped out heirs, bearing eleven children in their first fourteen years of marriage, five of them male. This was tough on her five-foot-tall body. By the time she was forty, she was emaciated, there were hairline fractures on her pelvis from the child-birthing, and her bones were deteriorating from the syphilis. She took a trip with her son Garzia to see her older son Giovanni in Pisa, even though he'd warned them there was a malaria outbreak. One by one, first Garzia, then Giovanni, then Eleonora succumbed to the disease and died. From the looks of the dress, her funeral must have been grand.

Right down the steps from the gallery is the wondrous expanse of the Boboli Gardens. In the warmer months, you can stroll paths bordered by lemon trees and blooming flowerbeds, just as Eleonora did.

Pitti Palace: Houses the Palatine Gallery, Gallery of Modern Art, Porcelein Museum, Boboli Gardens, and the Costume Gallery. Costume Gallery open daily 8:15-4:30 or -6:30, depending on the season. Closed first and last Mondays of the month. (www.polomuseale.firenze.it)

❧

Golden Day: Enjoy wandering around the **Costume Gallery** and **Boboli Gardens**, linger in the **Oltrarno** with lunch nearby at **Ristorante Ricchi** (Piazza Santo Spirito 8/r, 055 215 864), where you can sit outside and enjoy the view of Santo Spirito, with specialties such as *pappardelle al ragu di cinghiale* (pasta with wild boar tomato sauce).

TIP: *Your entrance to the Costume Gallery also includes admission to the nearby* **Giardini Bardini** *(www.bardinipeyron.it), which can be reached through the Boboli Gardens. So if it's a beautiful day, especially in springtime, include a stop at these quieter gardens and enjoy lovely views of Florence.*

RECOMMENDED READING

The House of Medici, Its Rise and Fall by Christopher Hibbert

24 Palazzo Davanzati

ONCE UPON A TIME, in fourteenth-century Florence, rich folks lived in tower houses. Entering Palazzo Davanzati is stepping back into that fairy tale time. Four floors have been restored into a **Museum of the Old Florentine House**, a family home complete with intriguing details—including kitchen gadgets, an ingenious plumbing system, and bedrooms with ensuite bathrooms and toilets. Then there are the trap doors where hot oil was poured to defend against attackers, along with displays of delicate lace. It's fascinating to see the backstage of the characters you see in the paintings in Florence's galleries.

The Davanzati family—wealthy, intellectual merchants—acquired the building in 1538. The original owners from medieval times had combined a few tower homes to create this wide one, and when the Davanzatis came in they added the top-floor open-air loggia where you can have a marvelous view of Florence. Over the years the palazzo was remodeled and damaged, until thankfully, in 1904, Elia Volpi, one of the greatest Italian antique collectors of the twentieth century, restored it to its medieval gothic style.

Volpi had aspired to be a painter, and when that didn't work out, he took the opportunities that came his way to acquire treasures from the many aristocratic families in the city who had fallen on hard economic times. Thus in 1910, with much fanfare, he transformed the palazzo into a Museo dell'Antica Casa Fiorentina—a showroom and store that introduced foreigners to the Florentine style. Among Volpi's customers was the American Art Academy, and many of the pieces he sold are now displayed at the Metropolitan Museum of Art and Frick Collection in New York.

The palazzo has been a state museum since 1956, and underwent an excellent restoration recently, turning it into one of Florence's most entertaining museum experiences, with guided tours by enthusiastic docents who bring bygone days to life.

There are impressive furnishings from various collections, along with antique ceramics, and the room's walls are painted in a fashion that resembles colorful tapestries—from medieval crests and geometric patterns, to more flamboyant versions such as the Pappagalli (parrots) and Pavoni (peacocks) rooms.

A favorite for the romantic in me is the **Camera della Castellana di Vergi**, a large bedroom painted to celebrate the marriage of Paolo Davanzati to Lisa degli Alberti in 1350. It features a frieze that tells the story of The Lady of Vergy—a popular epic poem of the day.

The plot is the stuff of juicy soap operas: A handsome knight and a married noble woman fall madly in love and begin a routine of secret trysts that involves the Lady sending her dog out to her garden as a sign that the coast is clear and the knight can safely enter her chamber. The course of romance does not run smoothly, when the Duchess of Burgundy makes a play for the handsome knight, and he rebuffs her, loyal to his lady love. The Duchess's revenge causes a tragic finale—the Lady dying of heartbreak when her secret affair is revealed, the knight stabbing himself over the Lady's dead body, the Duke beheading the Duchess for causing it all.

The most important collection in the palazzo is the Lace and Embroidery exhibit on the first floor. Beautiful pieces from the sixteenth to the twentieth centuries, made in Italy, Belgium, Britain, and America are exquisitely displayed in frames and glass sliding cases, inspiring hushed *oohs and ahhs*.

Palazzo Davanzati: Via di Porta Rossa 13, open daily 8:15–1:50, closed second and fourth Sundays, and first, third, and fifth Mondays of the month. Reservations needed in advance to tour upper floors at 10 A.M., 11 A.M., and noon, though I've had luck showing up a half hour before and signing up. (www.polomuseale.firenze.it)

❧

Golden Day: Follow your visit to the palazzo with lunch at the nearby **La Bussola**, a restaurant/wine bar/pizzeria, that offers excellent Tuscan specialties as well as fish. It's a perfect spot for the solo traveler, with seats at the bar where you can watch pizzas being made in the wood-burning oven. (Via Porta Rossa 58/r, 055 293 376, www.labussolafirenze.it)

TIP: *This is a great museum for families, fun for kids to roam about and imagine living in such a place!*

RECOMMENDED READING

Manners and Customs in the Middle Ages by Marsha Groves (part of Medieval World series for children)

25 Casa Guidi: Elizabeth Barrett Browning's Apartment

WHEN WE THINK OF "How do I love thee, Let me count the ways," Elizabeth Barrett Browning's most famous line, it seems only natural that this romantic poet would wind up in Italy. It was *amore* that brought her to Florence, where she lived for fourteen years with her husband Robert Browning. Stop by their former Oltrarno apartment to get a hit of what life was like for these bohemians back in the nineteenth century.

When Barrett met Browning in London, she was thirty-eight and at an all-time low. Her poetry books were a smash, but she was a semi-invalid with lung problems that began with a spinal injury she got as a teenager and left her dependent on opium for the rest of her life. And she was in mourning for her beloved brother. He'd gone with her to a lovely lakeside spot to help restore her health and then tragically drowned in that lake.

In swooped poet-on-the-rise Robert Browning, who wrote her a fan letter that began, "I love your verses with all my heart..." It was a little too over the top for Elizabeth, but the two started writing to each other and after a few months Robert showed up at her father's house, where she was living as a recluse. Robert was six years younger than Elizabeth, a strapping, healthy guy, and it was hard for her to even imagine he could love her. Elizabeth's wealthy, tyrannical father was dead set against any of his twelve children coupling, but after their first meeting, a secret romance between Elizabeth and Robert began.

A year later, in 1846, they eloped, and Robert whisked Elizabeth off to Italy for their honeymoon, along with her nurse and cocker spaniel. Elizabeth described it as "living a dream." After toodling around, they found this gem of a six-room apartment in Florence. They bargained with the landlord, giving him back the grand furniture the place came with, and getting the rent down to twenty-five guineas a year, which included free entrance to the nearby Boboli Gardens.

The apartment is on the *piano nobile* (what we think of as the second floor) of this fifteenth-century palazzo, once owned by Count Guidi. You pass through a big dining room to get to the main attraction: the drawing room where Elizabeth wrote and hung out with artists and writers like the Hawthornes and Harriet Beecher Stowe.

Thanks to an oil painting Robert had done, the room looks almost exactly as it was when the Barrett-Brownings lived here. It has a cozy Victorian style, with intense olive green walls, soft lighting, velvet upholstered furniture, and a little table with a mother of pearl tea set. In the middle of it all is a tiny writing desk where you can imagine Elizabeth composing *Aurora Leigh*—a love story of a woman writer making her way in the world. The gilt-framed mirror over the fireplace is the one piece that's original to Casa Guidi. Elizabeth wrote to her sister about how thrilled she was Robert bought it, even though to her the five-pound price was an extravagance.

Elizabeth got her strength back in Florence. At forty-three she gave birth to a son, whom she nicknamed Pen. She got passionately involved with the Italian fight for independence, and wrote the poem "Casa Guidi Windows" in support of the Florentines she saw from her terrace, who protested fiercely against Austrian occupation.

Though most biographies claim "they lived happily ever after," Elizabeth and Robert were real people, so it wasn't a fifteen-year honeymoon. Elizabeth was the poet star of the duo, paying all the bills for the house and many wonderful vacations, with her writing profits and money she'd inherited from an uncle. She got her way when it came to dressing Pen, outfitting him in effeminate velvet getups and having his hair grow in long curls like his mommy's. Robert didn't stand behind Elizabeth's passions—feminism, the fight for Italian unification, and most of all her explorations into spirituality, which involved consulting mediums. Add to that her four miscarriages and opium addiction to give some shadings to the "happily ever after" story.

A photograph of Elizabeth just months before her death shows her dressed in billowing black silk, with that signature cascade of curls surrounding a face that looks pained and cadaverous. The story goes she died in Robert's arms in 1861 in Casa Guidi, at the age of fifty-five. Some suspect Robert may have upped the dose of morphine to put an end to her suffering.

Robert left Florence after Elizabeth died and never returned. In England, he finally reached his success as a poet.

In Elizabeth's memory (no mention of Robert), the Florentines placed a plaque over the doorway of the Casa Guidi apartment building, honoring her for poetry they said "made a golden ring between Italy and England."

Casa Guidi: Piazza San Felice 8 (Oltrarno), Monday, Wednesday, Friday, 3-6, April 1 to November 30 (www.browningsociety.org). **English Cemetery:** Piazzale Donatello, for Elizabeth Barrett Browning's grave.

≈

Golden Day: Visit **Casa Guidi**, enjoy the **Oltrarno**. Have dinner at **Osteria del Cinghiale Bianco**, set in a thirteenth-century tower, serving robust versions of traditional Florentine dishes. (Borgo San Iacopo 43, 055 215706, closed Wednesday, open for dinner on weeknights and lunch only on Saturday and Sunday, www.cinghialebianco.com)

TIP: *The attached rooms of the Barrett-Browning place that aren't being used for a museum have been turned into a vacation apartment, so you can sleep where the Brownings slept. It's three bedrooms, three bathrooms, and kitchen. (www .landmarktrust.org.uk)*

RECOMMENDED READING

Elizabeth Barrett Browning by John Henry Ingram

26 Taste Florence

THE WORLD HAS FALLEN IN LOVE with the wonderful wines of Tuscany and the simple cuisine of the region. Meals in Florence are inspired by Tuscany's abundant farms, featuring delicious vegetables, beef from prized Chianina cattle, along with extraordinary olive oil and cheeses.

Traditional dishes to order are:

* **Antipasti**: *Affetati* (a mixed plate of salamis and cheeses), *crostini di fegatini* (toasted bread with chicken liver pate), *fettunta* (toasted bread with garlic and oil)
* **Pasta**: *al pomodoro* (with tomato sauce), *al cinghiale* (wild boar sauce), *ai funghi* (mushroom sauce)
* **Vegetables**: *Ribollita* (soup with bread, beans, and vegetables), *Panzanella* (salad of bread, tomato, and vegetables of the season), *Fagioli all'uccelletto* (beans stewed with sage and tomato)
* **Meat**: *Bistecca alla Fiorentina* (grilled steak, always served rare), *Tagliata* (sliced beef), *Trippa* (tripe), *Pollo alla Diavola* (grilled, flattened chicken)
* **Dolce**: *Cantucci con Vin Santo* (biscotti served with sweet desert wine)

My Favorite Restaurant

❊ **Sostanza,** Via Porcellana 25r, 055 212 691, reservations essential, closed Saturday and Sunday
This down-to-earth trattoria has been around since 1869 and is always packed with locals and travelers, many who have been coming here for generations. Order their specialty starter, *tortino di carciofi* (artichoke flan), followed by *bistecca* and chicken cooked in butter, and save room for the meringue cake dessert. There are two dinner times, 7:30 and 9:45, where you're seated at communal tables in the white-tiled dining room. It's a great spot for solo travelers—I've always met wonderful people here—all of us reveling in the lively atmosphere and outstanding flavors.

Caffès

❊ **Caffè Gilli,** Piazza della Repubblica 36-39r
This began as a confectioner's shop in 1733, and moved to this central piazza in the early 1900s. Now it's an elegant place to have your espresso in airy *belle époque* surroundings, served by waiters in crisp white jackets. Their chocolates and pastries are *delizioso*.

❊ **Gran Caffè Giubbe Rosse,** Piazza della Repubblica 13/14R
A *caffè storico letterario* (historic literary caffè) where the Italian futurist movement blossomed in the early twentieth century. It's traditionally been a meeting place for intellectuals from around the world, and hosts book signings, art exhibits, and performances. Dark wood, marble tables, and tiled floors mix to create a warm, welcoming Old World atmosphere.

● **Caffè Cibreo**, Via Andrea del Verrocchio 5r (near Sant'
Ambrogio market)
Superstar chef Fabbio Picchi reigns at a group of award-winning restaurants clustered here—Cibreo, Trattoria Cibreo,
Teatro del Sale (a dinner theatre), and this beautiful
caffè. It's perfect for a pick me up on your way to the Sant'
Ambrogio market, though you may want to linger and
indulge in their outstanding selection of pastries . . . and you
may even be tempted to stay for lunch.

Gelato

● **Gelateria dei Neri,** Via dei Neri 20-22r (near Santa Croce)
A *signor* who once ran the revered Vivoli now runs this
little place nearby, serving great fruit flavors and delicious
profiteroles.

● **Caffè delle Carrozze,** Piazza del Pesce 3-5/r (near Ponte
Vecchio)
The location may seem too good to be true, but whenever
I ask locals "Where's the best gelato?" "Carrozze" is their
answer. From what I've tasted, they're absolutely right. The
fruit flavors change with the seasons, and the charming staff
is sweet about offering tastes to help you decide what to order.

● **La Carraia,** Piazza Nazario Sauro (just over Ponte Carraia
on Oltrarno side) and Via Benci 24/r (near Santa Croce)
Another local favorite where the prices are low and quality
is tops.

Chocolate

* **Vestri,** Borgo degli Albizi 11r (near Santa Croce)
There's a lively energy at this tiny shop where *molto bello* owner Leonardo doles out artisan chocolates that include unusual creations made with flavors like Earl Grey and chile. Wonderful stop for hot chocolate in the winter, *and* the gelato here is *fantastico*,  which you should order *affogato*, topped with their to-die-for hot chocolate sauce. Candies are packaged in Tiffany-blue boxes and make great gifts.

Wine Bars

What with all those wonderful vineyards surrounding the city, Florence has a long-standing tradition of wine shops that would always serve their customers glasses of *vino* and snacks. These old-style wine bars are called *fiaschetteria*, from the word *fiasche*, meaning straw-covered chianti bottles. (I'll date myself with the sweet memory of turning those bottles into candlesticks to add a romantic touch to a dorm room.) Whether you get to a *fiaschetteria* or newer place, you'll be drinking some of the best wines in Italy and eating delectable Tuscan cheeses, salamis, and panini.

* **Casa del Vino**, Via dell'Ariento 16/r (San Lorenzo), closed Sunday all year and Saturdays June through September
This humble place, tucked behind the San Lorenzo Market, hasn't changed since I first walked in more than twenty years ago. Then I stood alongside the workmen, had a tumbler of wine and anchovy panini, and got an ecstatic feeling that I'd

discovered a hidden treasure. It's in every guidebook now and gets crowded with tourists. But the Migliorini family, who have owned it for seventy years, keeps things traditional, and those delicious panini continue to be a not-to-be-missed Florentine treat.

* **Le Volpi e L'Uva**, Piazza de' Rossi 1, open 11-9
The sommelier and his partners who run this place are committed to be like *volpi* (foxes) and seek out new, high-quality, small wine producers. Get in on their discoveries that you'll enjoy with gourmet nibbles: delicious cheeses and cured Tuscan meats.

* **Fuori Porta**, Via del Monte all Croci 10r, open daily 12:30-midnight
A perfect stop after a sunset walk to Piazzale Michelangelo, this casual place has an outstanding selection of wines from all over Italy and beyond. It gets packed with locals at dinner, and also serves delicious small plates of Tuscan specialties, salads, and homemade cakes.

Wine Bar, Caffè, and Bakery

* **Cantinetta Verrazano**, Via dei Tavolini 18/r, Monday-Saturday 8-9, Sunday 10-4:30
A delicious find between the Duomo and Piazza Signoria. It's a restored Florentine bakery, taken over by the family who owns the esteemed Verrazano winery in Chianti. One side is a bakery with the original woodburning oven, turning out delicious focaccia, pastries, and cookies, served with Piansa

coffee (Florence's best). On the other side, you can sit and taste award-winning wines with delicious Tuscan snacks.

RESOURCES FOR EATING IN FLORENCE

The Curious Eater: www.thecuriouseater.com

Divina Cucina: www.divinacucina.com (Click **About Judy** to find her "Florence for Foodies" recommendations)

27
Backstage at Il Mercato Centrale

THE **MERCATO CENTRALE DI SAN LORENZO** is a food market so revered by the Florentines that it's overseen by the same art commission that looks after the Uffizi galleries. The vast glass and cast-iron structure from 1865 is one of the oldest and biggest markets in Italy. Its top floor was recently renovated into an enticing food court, and throughout you're surrounded by mouth-watering temptations: wheels of fragrant pecorino cheese, tubs of grapes, shelves glowing with bottles of olive oil, stuffed pig heads.

It's as overwhelming as a Florentine gallery, which is why I signed up with an expert foodie guide, Judy Witts-Francini, to delve deeper into the finest treasures to be found here.

Judy's been shopping here since 1984. That was the year she left her job as a pastry chef in San Francisco and moved to Florence. She arrived not knowing a soul and didn't speak a word of Italian. It was at the Mercato Centrale where she learned the language—talking to the vendors, hearing their recipes, eavesdropping on conversations. Falling in love and marrying a Florentine, Andrea Francini, soon followed.

Though she's studied professionally and is a member of top international chef associations, Judy tells me her best teacher was her Florentine mother-in-law: "She taught me the most important thing about Italian cooking: *Spend more time shopping and less time cooking.* It's not the recipe or the time you spend in the kitchen that makes good food. It's the quality of the ingredients you work with. In Italian they say: *"la material prima."*

"Taste this," she says, as we stand in front of the counter of one of her friends' shops. It's twelve-year-old balsamic vinegar that wakes up every taste bud. That's just the opener to Judy's tour of one refined taste after another: twenty-five-year-old balsamic, pecorino cheese with truffle honey, olive oil fresh from the press. We continue our stroll, and I get her insider's generous scoop along the way: *That's where to go for the best panini, stop here for spices, there's my favorite butcher...*

Judy's passion for the details of it all is infectious, and she's an absolutely delightful person to be with. Though she's lived in Florence most of her life, her drive and pioneering spirit are a reflection of her California roots. She was part of the first wave of expats setting up travel businesses and websites in Italy (in the 1990s) and has expanded her successful company, **Divina Cucina**, to offer cooking classes in the Tuscan countryside as well as in Sicily, and she's written a travel app for touring Chianti.

Heading out of the market for lunch at nearby Mario's, we make a final stop at **Pork's**, one of the many restaurant stands on the lower level. This one has been run by a Sicilian family for over twenty years.

"Meet my market Mamma," Judy says, introducing me to Benita, the Pork's matriarch—a seventy-something-year-old *signora* with a jet-black bouffant hair-do.

Benita stands proudly in front of her case of food: *eggplant caponata, arancine*. Within five minutes, she's insisted on sitting us down with a plate of "tastings," even though we keep telling her we're off to lunch. Without Judy, I would have passed this by, thinking: *Why a Sicilian restaurant in Florence?* Why? Because the flavors are out of this world.

Pork's is now my go-to lunch spot at the market. Benita is always there to welcome me back with a kiss and *caponata*. I savor the flavors and toast Judy for the bonus I got from her backstage tour: A little piece of family at the Mercato Centrale for many visits to come.

TOURS

Divina Cucina (www.divinacucina.com) offers Florence Market Tours, Culinary Adventures in Tuscany and Sicily, and restaurant advice.

RECOMMENDED READING

Secrets from My Tuscan Kitchen by Judy Witts-Francini

28 *Florence Spas and a Hair Salon*

Take a beauty break in this beautiful city.

* **Four Seasons Hotel Spa,** Borgo Pinti 99, 055 26261 (www.fourseasons.com/Florence)

   It's an absolute surprise to discover this luxury property off the quiet, narrow Borgo Pinti. The hotel is a splendidly renovated fifteenth-century palazzo, set on eleven acres of gorgeous green and garden, shaded by majestic centuries-old trees. The spa, in a separate, modern two-story building surrounded by botanical gardens, keeps up the elegant flow, with a staff of experts giving sophisticated service. Signature treatments blend with Florence—such as *Iris Sensations* (using the rejuvenating powder from the flower that symbolizes Florence), *Chianti Wine Massage*, and facials using products from the *Officina Profumo Farmaceutica di Santa Maria Novella*. There are even Teen massages, and a Full-Time Mom treatment can be custom designed for mothers and children to relax together. Afterward, you can bliss out by the garden pool and have lunch or an aperitivo at the **Al Fresco** restaurant. If you're up for a splurge, this is your spot.

* **Klab,** Via de' Conti 7, 055 215 902
  Conveniently located near Piazza Duomo, this huge, modern fitness center has all you need to stay on your healthy
  track and get a little pampering: fully equipped gym, sauna,
  Turkish bath, massages, facials, yoga, Pilates, or aerobics
  class.

Hair Salon

* **Simonetta Pini,** Viale Antonio Gramsci 27, 055 247 7713
  How lovely it is to slip into this lively salon, joining in with
  Simonetta's loyal followers: beautiful Florentine women who
  have been coming here for decades. Simonetta gives excep-
  tional cuts, the colorists are great, and you could also get
  your nails done.

29 A Walk and a Bike Ride in Florence

Walk to Piazzale Michelangelo

If you reach the Piazzale Michelangelo at sunset, when the sky does that great show of gold-turquoise-rose, you realize that the Renaissance painters weren't making anything up—the light here is simply that magical. The panoramic view is one of the most photographed in the world: Arno, Ponte Vecchio, Duomo, red rooftops...

The climb up the winding pathways and steps to get there is well worth the effort, taking about half an hour, depending on your pace. My walk begins by crossing over the Ponte delle Grazie (near Santa Croce) to Via di San Niccolo, then up to the gate in the old city walls (Porta San Miniato). From there you continue left and can detour to the Rose Garden, for a relaxing break on the grass, surrounded by fragrant blooms and the recent addition of bronze statues by the surrealist Belgian artist, Jean-Michel Folon, adding a unique touch to the landscape. If you're there in May, the Iris Garden next to it will be open, with splendid displays of violets, golds, and blues—a tribute to the flower that symbolizes Florence.

Up at the Piazzale, there might be a mob scene of tourists, buses, and schlocky souvenir stands, but there's plenty of space for you to find a spot away from that and take in your reward of a view. The Piazzale was built in 1869 when Florence became the capital of Italy. The original plan was to make it a Michelangelo tribute, with bronze casts of his sculptures up there. They only made it as far as the *David*, and the museum that was to hold the art became La Loggia caffè, a good place for a *caffè* or cocktail... but not recommended for eating!

Go farther uphill to discover one of the oldest churches in Florence: **San Miniato al Monte**. It was named in honor of Minas, an Armenian Prince, who was beheaded for his Christian beliefs. Apparently that didn't faze him—the story goes that he simply carried his head across the Arno and up this hill.

The church façade is done up in pretty green and white marble, Santa Maria Novella style, and the cavernous inside has a cool, evocative vibe, with thirteenth-century mosaics at the altar and beautiful frescos by Taddeo Gaddi, a student of Giotto. If your timing is right (usually at 10 A.M. and 5:30 P.M.), you'll hear the Benedictine monks singing vespers, their voices echoing off the stones. Their monastery is next door, as well as their *farmacia*, selling their handmade candles, jams, and liqueurs.

San Miniato al Monte, Via delle Porte Sante 34, open daily 7 till sunset, in winter closed 1-3:30 (www.sanminiatoalmonte.it)
Farmacia Monastica (Next to San Miniato al Monte), open daily 10-12:15, 3:30-6

Biking in Florence with Florencetown

The historic center of Florence—a flat, cobblestoned, pedestrian-only zone—seems perfect for biking. It certainly is, if you know your way around the zig-zag of streets, the tourist crowds, and licensed vehicles that may pop up by surprise. If you're new here, signing up for a guided bike tour with **Florencetown** is the best way to blend in with the local cycling culture. You're set up with vintage bikes, complete with bells and baskets, as well as a headset, to get directions and com-  mentary. Over the next two and a half hours, the charming, native guide stops you at key spots along the way, to share his or her passion and knowledge of Florentine history. It's a great way to orient yourself when you arrive, and it ends with a free gelato. All touring should be this much fun.

Bike Tours with Florencetown: www.florencetown.com

Golden Day: Time your walk to get to **Piazzale Michelangelo** for the sunset, with a leisurely stop at the Rose Garden and a look around San Miniato. On the walk down, stop in at the **Fuori Porta** wine bar, where you'll have an extensive choice of wines by the glass and can enjoy delicious Tuscan cheeses and salami. (Via Monte alle Croce 10r, open daily 12:30-midnight)

30

Learn Florentine Artisan Crafts

WITH SO MANY WONDERFUL ARTISANS in Florence, there are opportunities for you to become an apprentice to a master, joining in on traditions of craftsmanship that have been practiced here for centuries. You can sign on for a taste of it for a few hours, or immerse yourself in the hands-on experience for weeks, or as long as you wish.

Some suggestions:

Leather Making at Scuola del Cuoio

A morning at **Scuola del Cuoio** taught me the true meaning of "tough as leather." Believe me, I learned from my class that a bad steak is a cinch to cut compared to the leather journal cover I labored over at the *scuola* for an entire morning. Forever I am grateful to my teacher, master Carlo, *Papa Patience,* who guided me step by step through the challenge that ended with triumph: a souvenir journal that brings back fond memories of Florence.

The *scuola* is in a building that was a monastery in Renaissance days, tucked behind the Santa Croce church, in an area where leather making in Florence first began. It was founded by the Gori family in 1950, as an artisans' school for boys who'd been orphaned after World War II. The goal was to teach them a trade so they could earn a practical living. The Goris teamed up with

Franciscan friars to create the scuola, turning the monk's dormitories into a workshop. And not just any old dormitory—it was built by the Medici in the fifteenth century. The upstairs section, open to visitors, is a gorgeous fresco-lined hall, where senior artisans at old-fashioned wooden workstations turn out some of the best handcrafted leather to be found in Florence, which, by the way, is conveniently for sale in the adjoining rooms. The descendants of the founder—three elegant Gori daughters and a grandson—expertly run the place.

Downstairs is the workshop, where my lesson took place, amidst the pros and some other students. Across the room from me were two happy American gals, here for the scuola's longer programs (three months), who were turning out adorable purses.

Once I got the slowed down pace of the process, I fell into my hours there, with *pazienza, pazienza, pazienza*. Cutting the leather was the hardest, and then Carlo took me through each step that followed, with exacting instructions for folding, pressing, hammering holes along the border.

After the days I'd spent running around Florence, looking at stupendous masterpieces, this detailed work took me into another dimension. As I sat there, focused on pulling one thin strip of leather through tiny holes of the journal cover to make a braided edge, I gave in to "leather-crafting" time. The room had an overwhelming scale of aromas—from the deep smell of leather to top notes of nose-tingling glue. Church bells rang. It was simply divine to be there.

My journal cover finished, Carlo gave me a warm "Congratulations," filled it with fine blank Florentine paper, then walked me to a workbench where Bosco, a venerable, bald-headed artisan, performed his magic over it—with egg white, a flame, and twenty-two-carat gold. He handed it back to me, transformed: with my embossed initials in gold—a lasting reward for hours of *pazienza, pazienza.*

Scuola del Cuoio, Piazza di Santa Croce 16, 055 244 533 Half-day, full-day, three-month, and six-month courses. This is also a great place to see artisans at work and buy beautiful handcrafted leather, particularly handbags. They also expertly tailor jackets and can custom make anything your heart desires. (www.scuoladelcuoio.com)

Jewel on the Arno/Jewelry Courses in Florence

Ken Scott, originally from New Zealand, is an artisan who has worked for major jewelry companies in Florence for fourteen years. He has also branched out on his own, creating an exquisite jewelry line, and teaches the craft at Florence's prestigious professional institutions. Recently he opened his own workshop/school, in a well-equipped studio, where students can come for programs (from two weeks to three months), learn about the history of jewelry making in Florence, and receive individual instruction—depending on their level—to master the art of jewelry making.

As Ken puts it: "The purpose is not to learn just how to make jewelry, but how to become a jeweler." He's praised by his students for his great sense of humor and expert attention and guidance.

Jewel on the Arno: www.kenscottdesign.com

31 *Shopping in Florence*

FLORENCE IS HEAVEN FOR SHOPPERS. Within a small, easily walkable area, it offers luxury to artisan treasures, along with outdoor markets where you can bargain for scarves, leather, and kitschy souvenirs.

Via Tornabuoni is the center for high-end fashion, with such designers as **Emilio Pucci, Giorgio Armani,** and **Gucci.** To get more **Gucci,** visit the **Gucci Museo** on nearby Piazza Signoria, where you'll find displays documenting the history of the fashion powerhouse, a shop that custom makes purses, and a chic Restaurant and Caffè.

Gucci Museo: Piazza Signoria 10, open 10-8, Restaurant/ Caffè 10-11 (www.guccimuseo.com)

My favorite on the Via Tornabuoni stretch is:

Ferragamo Museum and Store
Come here to marvel over the creations of Salvatore Ferragamo, who was the grandpapa of modern Italian shoe fashion. These days his widow Wanda is queen of the company. She's so beloved by Italians they've even named a rose in her honor.

The shop is in a medieval palace that Ferragamo bought in 1938, after his rise to success in Hollywood, designing shoes for movies such as *The Ten Commandments*. Actresses clamored for his creations to wear off the set, and he became "The Shoemaker to the Stars." What's always separated Ferragamo's shoes from the pack is that he consistently combined glamour with comfort. He was so obsessed he even took anatomy classes at the University of Southern California, so he could learn all about the foot.

The **Ferragamo Museum**, in the lower level of the store, pays homage to Salvatore with fantastic displays and photos of celebrities showing off his shoes—from Carmen Miranda to Katharine Hepburn to Andy Warhol. A video tells the story of Ferragamo's life—a man of humble beginnings from a village in southern Italy, who created what has become a fashion empire.

Shopping upstairs from the museum is a treat, especially in the boutique, where you'll find limited edition copies of such beauties as the heels Ferragamo designed for Marilyn Monroe for *Some Like It Hot*. And you may even see Wanda, who regularly stops by.

Ferragamo Museum and Store: Piazza Santa Trinita 5, open daily: 10-6 (www.museoferragamo.it)

Artisan Shopping, a few of my favorite things:

Beauty Products

* **Officina Profumo Farmaceutica di Santa Maria Novella,** Via della Scala 16, near Santa Maria Novella, open daily 9-8 (www.smnovella.it)

  Don't miss this place. Here gorgeously frescoed ceilings, sculpted columns and arches, stained glass windows, and a staff dressed in chic black takes a shopping experience to a mystical level.

The shop was a fourteenth-century Gothic church of Dominican friars, which was turned into a *farmacia* to sell their potions in 1612. Today scent scientists reproduce the monk's recipes, and their creations are shipped all over the world.

Santa Maria Novella potpourri, a blend of ten different herbs and flowers from the surrounding hills, comes in monogrammed satin pouches and makes a perfect gift. The top perfume choice is Acqua di Colonia, a citrus and bergamot blend created for Catherine de' Medici when she went off to Paris to marry Henry II. There's also Acqua di Santa Maria Novella (aka anti-hysteria water), which was created when tight-corset-wearing gals needed relief from the vapors. It's now recommended as a digestive aid.

Jewelry

❀ **Angela Caputi,** Via di Santo Spirito 58r (Oltrarno) and Borgo SS. Apostoli 44/46 (www.angelacaputi.com)
Caputi is a bold designer, who has rocked the high fashion world since 1975 with her unique, plastique jewelry. Both stores are delightfully welcoming, and it's a joy to be surrounded by her fun, vibrant bangles and necklaces.

❀ **Fratelli Piccini,** Ponte Vecchio 23
(www.fratellipiccini.com)
All the jewelry shops on the Ponte Vecchio used to be vegetable and fish stalls. Then the Medicis decided to build the Vasari corridor over the bridge to connect their two palaces.

"That stench!" they said to the merchants, kicked them out, and replaced them with goldsmiths. These days, according to Florentines, the only place to shop among the bridge's many choices is Fratelli Piccini, owned by the same family since 1903.

● **Museo Bottega del Maestro Alessandro Dari**, Via S. Niccolo 115, Oltrarno (www.alessandrodari.com)
As I walked by the fifteenth-century building that's home to Dari's shop, I was drawn inside by the sounds of a classical guitar. The player was the master goldsmith Alessandro Dari himself, sitting there in a muscle shirt, surrounded by cases of his jewelry, inspired by Florentine architecture. His rings and pendants, shaped like domes or castles and studded with gems, are extraordinary.

Ceramics

● **Sbigoli**, Via Sant Egidio 4/r (www.sbigoliterrecotte.it)
Colorful hand-painted designs (inspired by Renaissance tradition or modern twists) adorn the enticing displays of ceramics in this family run shop. You can see artisans in action in the back workshop, and they also offer classes for groups to get hands-on experience of ceramic making.

● **La Botteghina del Ceramista**, Via Guelfa 5/r (www.labotteghinadelceramista.it)
Vibrant displays of hand-painted ceramics from all over Italy fill this tiny shop, including small items (coasters and wine stoppers) that make great quality souvenirs.

Leather

⚙ **Scuola del Cuoio,** Piazza Santa Croce 16
(www.scuoladelcuoio.com)
Tucked behind the Santa Croce church, this store and workshop was once a monastery built by the Medici. You can watch artisans at their workstations crafting leather goods, or, with torch in hand, magically embossing them with gold filigree. Everything for sale is of the highest quality, cut and sewn right here, using leather tanned from Tuscan experts. There are desk sets, wallets, jackets, and a great selection of purses. The expert staff offers custom design services to create anything you wish, and you can take classes here to learn more about the art of leather making.

⚙ **Cellerini,** Via del Sole 37/r (near Piazza Santa Maria Novella, www.cellerini.it)
Allessandra Cellerini carries on the tradition she learned from her father Silvano, who began leather crafting as a teenager in the 1940s. He continues to advise her and her assistants in this glamorous shop, where beautiful handbags, belts, and accessories inspire sighs.

Gloves

⚙ **Madova,** Via De' Guicciardini, 1R, Oltrarno, open 10:30-7,
· closed Sunday
The Donnini family has been creating leather gloves in Florence since 1919. Their tiny shop, just over the Ponte Vecchio, is crammed with beauteous cashmere and silk-lined leather gloves, that you'd pay twice the price for back home.

Shoes: Handmade

Calzature Francesco da Firenze, Via Santo Spirito 62r, open 10-1, 4-7:30, closed Sunday
Stop by this family-run Oltrarno shop for handmade shoes, or leather sandals that they can customize for you in 24 hours.

Lingerie, Lace, Embroidery

* **Grazia Giachi,** Via Borgo Ognissanti 37/r
(www.graziagiachi.it)
An adorable, shoebox-sized shop that sells handmade luxurious silk lingerie with accents of lace, children's wear, and reasonably priced embroidered tea towels and table linens. It's family run, under the direction of Grazia, who has been embroidering since the age of eight, and who also has a workshop and store in **Greve in Chianti**.

* **Loretta Caponi**, Piazza degli Antinori 4r
(www.lorettacaponi.com)
Wow! Seven glorious rooms in the former Palazzo Aldobrandini show off Loretta's awesome hand- and machine-made pieces—from table linens, outfits for newborns that make grandmamas melt, and elegant lingerie. Nicole Kidman and Madonna are fans.

Paper

* **Il Torchio,** Via de Bardi 17, San Niccolò
  (www.legatoriailtorchio.com)
  Artisan Erin Ciulla owns this enchanting, tiny store and
  workshop, with a fabulous line of journals, frames, and gorgeous paper, that's lower priced than most others in town.
  She's also expert at customizing products to suit your desires.

Outdoor markets offer leather goods, scarves, and cheap souvenirs. Be prepared for aggressive sales pitches as you walk along,
and if you're paying cash, go ahead and bargain:

* **San Lorenzo,** extending through the streets surrounding
  the Mercato Centrale

* **Mercato Nuovo (aka Straw Market, Mercato del
  Porcellino),** corner of Via Porta Rossa and Via Por Santa
  Maria, near Piazza della Repubblica
  The bronze wild boar statue here holds a tradition similar to
  Rome's Trevi Fountain: if you pet its snout, you are ensured
  a return to Florence.

* **Piazza Santo Spirito Antique Market,** second Sunday of
  the month

Slightly off the beaten track, where you'll find more locals:

* **Mercato di Sant'Ambrogio,** Piazza Ghiberti
  A fabulous food market, surrounded by stalls selling kitchen
  gadgets and bargain clothing, open Monday-Saturday, 7-2

- **Piazza Ciompi,** flea market with vintage items for treasure hunters, open Monday–Saturday, 9-7:30 and last Sunday of the month

※

Golden Day: Enjoy the Via Tornabuoni shopping scene and lunch at **Procacci,** a gem of a six-table wine bar/deli from 1885, famous for its truffle-based specialties. Have a panino slathered with truffle butter and glass of Antinori wine. Via de Tornabuoni 64, open 10-8, closed Sunday. (www.procacci1885.it)

32
Entertainment in Florence

A DREAM HAS COME TRUE FOR FLORENCE: the opening of the **Nuovo Teatro dell'Opera**, a venue that's been praised as "the most avant garde opera house in the world." It's the new home of **Maggio Musicale Fiorentino**, Italy's oldest arts festival (www.operadifirenze.it), that now has an extended season of opera, music, and dance—so check the website to see what will be playing when you're there. Another big theater in the historic center is **Teatro Verdi** (www.teatroverdionline.com), which presents everything from visiting symphony orchestras, to Broadway shows, and children's theater.

Like Rome and Venice, Florence also has a tradition of excellent chamber orchestras performing in churches. Some favorite intimate venues for music are:

Classical Music and Opera

❋ **Orchestra da Camera Fiorentina—Chiesa di Orsanmichele** Critically acclaimed as the best chamber orchestra in Europe, this forty-piece ensemble performs chamber music and symphonic concerts, from such composers as Pergolesi, Schubert, Beethoven, and Haydn. Star guest musicians often add flash to the bill. It's on a grander scale than most "music in churches" experiences, but fitting for the vast Orsanmichele, a granary turned Gothic sanctuary. Performances take place March through October. (www.orcafi.it)

❀ **Opera at Saint Mark's English Church**
No binoculars are needed for the operas that are performed in this church that was once part of a Medici palace. Four or five top singers perform evenings of classics—including *La Traviata, Boheme,* or *Carmen,* and also concerts of opera duets. The acoustics are great and drinks are served at intermission—it's an experience that has been known to convert "I hate opera" people. (www.concertoclassico.blogspot.com)

❀ **Amici della Musica** is an organization that presents chamber music at the seventeenth-century jewel box in the Oltrarno, **Teatro della Pergola**, or a smaller former ballroom, the **Salonico**, beloved by soloists for its excellent acoustics. (www.amicimusica.fi.it)

Jazz

❀ **Jazz Club Firenze**
You'll be mixing with the locals for a bargain here—a five euro cover gets you a table and your first drink. Shows change nightly—from jazz jams to blues to folk. Snacks only served in a warm, welcoming atmosphere. (Via Nuova de Caccini 3, shows start at 10:30 P.M.-5 A.M., Tuesday-Sunday, 339 498 0752)

* **Golden View Open Bar**

 Cocktails, jazz, and great views of the moonlight shimmering on the Arno. Yes, it's packed with tour– ists and a bit pricier  than other places, but the music quality is high and the location perfect. (Via de Bardi 58, 055 214 502, Jazz on Monday, Wednesday, Friday, and Saturday starting at 9 P.M. If you're having dinner, reservations are recommended. www .goldenviewopenbar.com)

For entertainment listings:
www.theflorentine.net, www.firenzeturismo.it

Side Trips
from Florence

Gardens Outside Florence

LEAVE THE VESPA ROARS OF FLORENCE behind and head to the surrounding hills to discover lovely small gardens with fabulous views. Here's where Florentines have come to relax since the days of the Medici.

These are two that you can get to easily from Florence, by taking a short bus ride and walking about ten minutes. If you're feeling energetic, you could even hike up to them from the city, just like folks in olden days.

Villa Medici—Fiesole

Three terraces of simple grace make up Italy's first Renaissance garden.

In 1461, Giovanni de Medici, the son of Cosimo, bought this land because he loved the view of the city below. His dad thought it was a cockamamie idea: Why spend a bundle for a steep, rocky plot that you can't even grow anything on? The Medici were originally farming people, and Papa Cosimo's beloved spot was his country villa, where he'd tend vineyards and olive groves, hang with the peasants, and have friends over to read Plato.

His son Giovanni, a Medici banker, was of the new generation. Inspired by Pliny's ancient Roman writings, he got the notion that a garden was a place to combine home, nature, and an awesome view. Forget about growing food. Forget about the walled medieval garden. His terraces would blend with the landscape and villa, like an outdoor room. This would be a beautiful place to kick back, enjoy entertainments, and contemplate the mysteries of life.

Tall cypress trees line the entrance and pots of lemon trees are neatly arranged on the front lawn. Giovanni brought in lemons from Naples in homage to the mythological Garden of Hesperides. According to Greek legend, the earth mother Gaia gave this magical garden to Hera on her wedding day, when she married  Zeus. In it was a tree bearing golden immortality-giving apples, guarded by Hesperides—nymphs of the night. In later years it was thought these apples were actually citrus fruits, thus all these lemons.

Giovanni's overeating and drinking got the better of him and he died of a heart attack in his forties before he had much time to enjoy this place. His nephew, Lorenzo the Magnificent, took it over, and it became a meeting place for the Neo-Platonic Academy. Here was where Lorenzo would lead philosophical discussions centered on the idea that perfection and happiness could be attained right here on earth (not in the afterlife) through intellectual contemplation and the appreciation of beauty. Lorenzo's artist friends—Michelangelo, Leonardo da Vinci, and Botticelli—along with philosophers, poets, and musicians were invited. You can imagine him in these gardens leading the group, with the glorious view of Florence in the background: "Play the lute! Read me a verse from the *Aeneid*! What's life's highest vocation? Tell me your ideas!"

Villa Medici: Via Beato Angelico 35, Fiesole (055 597 252) The gardens can be visited by appointment only.

How to get there: Bus #7 from the Stazione Centrale di Santa Maria Novella, Piazza San Marco, or the Duomo, to Fiesole's Piazza Mino, then an uphill walk.

Villa Gamberaia—Settignano

This place is so pretty it makes me feel prettier when I step into it. Landscape architects come here to study it. Painting classes set up their easels on the grounds. It's a vision of exquisite harmony: Cypress trees are immaculately clipped into soft, rounded shapes and archways. Crisp boxwood shrubs line rectangular reflecting pools. Pink roses tumble from trellises. A baroque stone niche embedded with shells and fossils holds a statue of Neptune. A greenest of green alley of grass stretches out to a low stone wall. That's your photo op perch, with a dreamy view of Florence in the background.

All this on only three acres! A graceful mix of Italian Baroque and Formal English styles.

The garden was first put together in the eighteenth century, when those grottoes were built. Then in 1895 came Romanian Princess Jeanne Ghyka, part of the wave of foreigners who descended on Florence in those days. She made the garden her pet project, tearing out the raised flowerbeds and replacing them with the oblong reflecting pools. She was a mysterious sort, only occasionally having guests in for tea, and neighbors knew little about her except that she lived with an American companion, Miss Blood. In 1925, a widow from Detroit who'd been married to a German baron took over and she, Baroness Von Ketteler, is the one who's responsible for the amazing topiary that gives this garden such a distinct character.

It was almost completely destroyed in World War II, and then bought by the industrialist Marcello Marchi, who restored it. Still run by his family, the villa's been converted to guest accommodations. To stay here is a dream. Or just get here in April, when the blooming pink azaleas are a quasi-psychedelic vision.

Villa Gamberaia: Via del Rossellino 72, Settignano, open daily 9-6 by appointment, 055 697 205 (www.villagamberaia.com)
How to get there: Bus #10 from Santa Maria Novella or San Marco to Settignano.

❧

Golden Day: See the **Villa Medici Gardens** and explore the treasures of **Fiesole**—the Roman Theater and Duomo. Lunch at the loggia of **Villa San Michele**, a former convent with a facade designed by Michelangelo that has become a romantic luxury hotel. Views from the restaurant are transcendent, the food refined and delicious. (Via Doccia 4, 055 567 8200, www.villasanmichele.com)

RECOMMENDED READING

Italian Gardens: A Guide by Helen Attlee and Alex Ramsey

TOURS

One Step Closer (www.onestepcloser.net) is a Florence-based tour operator that provides arrangements for guided garden tours.

34 Prato: Home to Mary's Sacred Girdle and Salome Dancing

SALOME, THE BIBLE'S VIRGIN FLOOZY, fantastically frescoed by Fra Filippo Lippi, is the logo for the town of Prato, and it's well worth it to take the half-hour train ride from Florence to see it. This town first got on the tourist map back in medieval days when Mary's sacred girdle ended up here. In a classic example of Italians combining such concepts, both the Virgin Mother's Girdle and the Virgin Floozy can be found in one place: Prato's Romanesque Duomo.

Mary's girdle, kept locked in a sacred chapel, is nothing like the "this girdle is killing me" kind of my mother's day. It's a green belt that Mary untied when she ascended into heaven and threw to doubting Saint Thomas to prove that yes, it was she whooshing away.

The girdle was passed down to Thomas's disciples, and then to a Jerusalem priest who was married (aok back in those days) and had a gorgeous daughter. The priest disapproved of a merchant named Michael who fell in love with his daughter, but the girl's sympathetic mother helped the couple elope and threw in Mary's girdle as a dowry. Michael and his bride sailed from Jerusalem to Prato, where Michael slept with the girdle under his mattress to protect it, until on his deathbed he handed it over to a Prato priest. The Chapel of the Sacred Girdle is decorated with frescos that tell that whole story.

Five times a year, with much pomp and incense, Mary's girdle is taken from the chapel and shown to thousands. Because the event attracts more than the Duomo can hold, master sculptor Donatello sculpted a pulpit attached to the outside of the church, adorned with flying *putti*. There's a copy of the original pulpit up there now, but you can see Donatello's original in the attached museum.

The Duomo's main attraction, on the center altar, is Fra Filippo Lippi's cycle of The Life of John the Baptist, especially *The Feast of Herod*, featuring Salome.

As the Bible story goes, Salome danced so fabulously for her stepfather, King Herod, that he "was pleased" and told her he'd do anything for her. Salome didn't have an answer for Herod, being just a youngster who didn't really know what she wanted, so she asked her mother, Herodias, for advice. "Bring me John the Baptist's head on a platter," was her mother's demand.

Herod didn't want to have John's head cut off, but since he'd made that promise to Salome in front of everyone at his birthday party, he couldn't back down. He'd put John in prison because the holy man had called him and Herodias adulterers. Yes, it was true they'd had a wild affair when they were married to others, got divorced, and then became husband and wife. Herod didn't want to kill John the Baptist, who had so many followers. But he had wife Herodias to contend with, who was a more vengeful type and held quite the grudge.

I blame Herodias for Salome going down in history as a bloodthirsty whore, when actually she was just a naïve Shirley Temple-like ten-year-old, who didn't have an answer to "your wish is my command." Over the years, Oscar Wilde and Hollywood screenwriters have taken Salome's story and spiced it up, so now her name brings visions of "The Dance of the Seven

Veils," and it's assumed Herod's "being pleased" meant she stripped for him.

In Lippi's image that follows Salome gracefully dancing, she's shown holding out the head of John the Baptist to her unfazed mother Herodias, surrounded by shocked spectators. Only Salome and Herod look straight out at the viewer, as if Lippi was guiding us to have compassion for these two.

It took Lippi thirteen years to finish these frescos, because he had major *amore* distractions from his work. While fresco-ing and friar-ing, he became smitten with Lucrezia Buti, a beautiful novice, and asked the nun's permission to use her for a model. Sparks flew in Lippi's studio, and during one of the Feasts of the Sacred Girdle when the whole town was partying, the two ran off together. Lucrezia got pregnant and gave birth to Filippino, who would also grow up to be a great painter. Because Lippi was so talented, and his patrons wanted to end the scandal, the Pope stepped in and gave Lippi and Lucrezia dispensation from their vows so they could marry. Lucrezia was Lippi's model for most of his masterpieces, which inspired Botticelli and Michelangelo.

A visit to this Duomo is not only a chance to enjoy Lippi's frescos; Prato is also a leisurely place to wander around with the locals, taste their famous *biscotti di Mattonella*, and get a break from the tourist crowds of Florence.

Duomo: Monday-Saturday 9-3, Sunday 10-4. **How to get there:** Train from Florence Santa Maria Novella station to the **Prato Porta al Serraglio Station** (half hour), then walk a few blocks to the **Duomo**.

৵৻

Golden Day: Go to Prato's Duomo to see Lippi's masterpiece. Have lunch at **La Vecchia Cucina di Soldano**, a cozy budget place that is packed with locals. (Via Pomeria 23, 0574 34665, closed Sunday, www.trattoriasoldano.it)

TIP: *If you're there September 8, you'll hit the town's biggest Sacred Girdle party of the year, with parades and festivities all over Prato. Other Sacred Girdle showings are Christmas, Easter, May 1, and August 15.*

Siena: City of Saint Catherine

THE EVENING SKY IN SIENA is a divine wonder to behold. Get a seat in the Piazza del Campo as the sun sets, and you're in for a show. Colors change from blue-pink-golden to a rich navy. Then out pop the stars. Whoever is doing the lighting here is brilliant.

Any time of day, Siena is one of the most pleasant cities to stroll around. You'll be awed by the Gothic **Duomo** outside and in. There's **Duccio's** *Maesta* (Majesty) in the **Museo dell'Opera Metropolitana**, where the BVM sits enthroned, holding a rose-robed baby Jesus, surrounded by twenty angels and nineteen saints. When this masterpiece was unveiled in 1310, the whole town came out with candles to ooh and aah over it as church bells rang.

All over Siena, Saint Catherine, the most important woman of the Middle Ages, is honored with statues, paintings, and altars. The beloved *Mystic of Politics* was born here in 1347, in the area called *Contrada dell'Oca*, or Neighborhood of the Goose.

Pilgrims flock to the church she went to while growing up, which is now the **San Domenico Basilica**. There you'll find the richly decorated Santa Caterina Chapel, with frescoes by Sodoma, who was a student of Leonardo da Vinci. In the center of it all is Catherine's head. Compared to a lot of other relics I've seen, it looks more like a mask, in amazing shape. Her thumb is nearby under a bell jar.

A short walk away is the **Casa Santuario di Santa Caterina**, where she was born and grew up. It doesn't look as it probably did in her day, as it's been transformed to a shrine with Renaissance paintings that tell stories from her life. But still, as you walk through what was her kitchen and go upstairs to her bedroom, you get a feel for the strong spirit of this brilliant woman. Get a load of the stone pillow she used–just one example of how she denounced creature comforts to feel closer to God.

Catherine was the twenty-fourth of twenty-five children, whose twin sister died in childbirth. She shocked her parents when she was seven and announced, "I've had a vision! I'm devoting my life to Christ!" Her mother tried to pull her away from her incessant praying and marry her off when she was twelve, but Catherine chopped off her hair and put up a fight. Her parents finally relented, and allowed her to join the Dominican nuns as a "tertiary," a lay person associated with the clergy.

Catherine dedicated herself to nursing the sick, but even the devout around her were concerned about her religious zeal, as she'd only eat communion wafers. These days, psychologists who've examined the lives of female saints focus on Catherine. They say she had survivor's guilt because of the death of her twin, and it manifested as what they call "holy anorexia nervosa."

Despite her diet, Catherine became a powerful, influential woman. She had a vision that set her on a path to change the world through letter writing. This was amazing, because she was illiterate. She dictated letters to her followers and sent them off to the Pope in Avignon, encouraging him to come back to Rome. Those fourteenth-century times were a mess with divisions in the papacy and Italy. Dante and Petrarch had written to Pope Gregory XI to try to get him to come back to Italy, but it was Catherine's outright begging, addressing the Pope as "sweet Babbo" (Sweet Daddy), and writing "Up father, like a man!" that got him to think about budging.

For the ultimate push, Catherine went on horseback to Avignon and had a one-on-one meeting that got the Pope to pull up stakes. He died shortly after, and Catherine joined the new pope in Rome, continuing to fight to unite the church through her writing. She died in Rome at thirty-three, of a paralytic stroke.

Catherine was canonized in 1461 as the Patron of Nurses and Fire Prevention. In 1939 she was named Co-Patron Saint of Italy (along with Saint Francis), in 1970 a Doctor of the Church, and in 1999, the Patron of Europe.

The Romans treasured her and have her body enshrined in the Santa Maria Sopra Minerva church, which coincidentally has a frescoed ceiling that resembles the Siena sky.

Catherine's head is in Siena, because, according to legend, it was stolen by Sienese. When Roman guards caught them leaving the city and asked the thieves to open their sack, it miraculously appeared to be full of rose petals. But when they got it back to Siena, the head re-appeared. Catherine's foot is now enshrined in Venice, at Santi Giovanni e Paolo. Everybody wanted a piece of this amazing woman. But you'll feel her presence living on most strongly in Siena.

Siena Duomo and Museo dell'Opera Metropolitana: Piazza Duomo 8, open March 1-November 2, 9:30-7, mid June-mid September 9:30-8, November 3-February 28, 9:30-5:30 (www.operaduomo.siena.it)

San Domenico Basilica: Piazza San Domenico, open 7-7

Casa Santuario di Santa Caterina: Costa di Sant'Antonio 6, open daily 9-1, 3-6:30 (www.arcidiocesi.siena.it)

How to get there: Easiest way is the bus from Florence, that takes about an hour and a half. The Florence SITA bus station is close to the train station, about a five-minute walk, to the right as you exit the train station. There is lots of room for luggage in a hold underneath the bus. www.sitabus.it

❧

Golden Day: Enjoy Siena and Saint Catherine sights. Get to the Campo for sunset. If you don't want to splurge at the obvious caffès, head to **Key Largo**, where you can head up a narrow stairway (more like a hole in the ceiling) with your glass of wine and wind up on a narrow wooden balcony to take in the whole scene. Eat nearby at **Ristorante Guidoriccio** (Via Giovanni Dupre 2, 0577 44350, closed Sunday) a restaurant that serves great pastas. Stay at **Palazzo Ravizza** (www.palazzoravizza.it), a restored Renaissance Palace.

III

Venice

"It is always assumed that Venice is the ideal place for a honeymoon. This is a grave error. To live in Venice or even to visit it means that you fall in love with the city itself. There is nothing left over in your heart for anyone else."
—Peggy Guggenheim

Venice is a sexy place. The curves of its Grand Canal and palazzos, mysterious passageways, flowing tides, even its nickname, *La Serenissima* (meaning The Most Serene), make it magically seductive.

It has always been closely tied to Mary and was officially established as an Italian republic on the same day as her Annunciation (March 25). It also has a history of being a bustling port town, and along with sailors and wealthy single merchants went prostitutes and high-class courtesans, like the famous poet Veronica Franco.

The mix of the Madonna and Working Girl aspects of Venice is literally carved in stone on the Rialto Bridge. On one side there's a bas-relief of the Annunciation. On the other side is a woman with her legs spread, sitting over flames. The story of this gal is that she was a prostitute who was around when the idea for building the Rialto Bridge was first proposed. "Impossible," she said. "If you build it, I'll burn my crotch!" And so the bridge was built and the bawdy woman remembered.

As far as the BVM in Venice, you'll be surrounded by masterpieces of architecture, painting, and sculpture that pay homage to Mary in Venetian Renaissance style, bringing out the vibrant, passionate emotions of her story.

You'll discover the *La Serenissima* side of Venice as you wander, get lost, and slip into her tranquil rhythms...surrounded by the ring of church bells, water lapping along the canals, seagulls swooping overhead...

Along with my suggestions, here are some major attractions:

Basilica San Marco: Where you'll find the extraordinary sparkling **Madonna di Nicopedia**, and upstairs the **Matroneum** (women's gallery)(www.basilicasanmarco.it)

Palazzo Ducale and Bridge of Sighs: See Tintoretto's *Triumph of Venice*, featuring the BVM, and imagine that notorious ladies' man, Casanova, crossing the Bridge of Sighs.

Gallerie dell' Accademia: Inside are beautiful Bellini Madonnas, Titian's *Presentation of the Virgin*, and the amazing Story of St. Ursula cycle by Carpaccio (www.gallerieaccademia.org)

TIP: *Speaking of Bellinis, a great place for cocktails is the Bar Longhi at the Gritti Palace Hotel (Campo Santa Maria del Giglio 2467, San Marco, 041 296 1222, www.thegrittipalace.com).*

RECOMMENDED READING

Venice by Jan Morris

The Honest Courtesan: Veronica Franco: Citizen and Writer in Sixteenth Century Venice by Margaret F. Rosenthal

36 *Santa Maria Churches in Venice*

FOR CENTURIES, VENETIANS BELIEVED THAT the Blessed Virgin Mother brought them miracles—from stopping a plague, to bringing fortune, to mysteriously appearing with advice. Many churches were built in honor of her powers. Among my favorites, by neighborhood, are:

Dorsoduro

* **Santa Maria della Salute**

    At the opening of the Grand Canal, *The Salute*, or what my husband calls "the giant white boob," welcomes visitors to Venice.

    Salute means health and salvation, which is what the Venetians needed desperately in 1631. For two years, the plague had ravaged the city, causing forty-five thousand deaths, a loss of one third of their population. The doge ordered prayers to Mary, the plague stopped, and it was decided to build a church to thank her.

    Baldassare Longhena, at thirty-two years old, won a contest to design the church and came up with a Mary-centric plan. The dome represents her crown, the round shape her womb, the octagonal interior, her eight-sided star. The center of the marble floor features thirty-two roses, symbolizing the beads of her Rosary.

It's refreshing to step into the airy expanse of this church, with loads of light flooding through its giant dome. A marble sculpture at the main altar tells the plague story. In the center is the Madonna and Child, bordered on one side by a pretty *signorina* who represents Venezia. On the other side is the plague—an old hag running from an angel who holds out a torch.

Pay the extra couple euros to get into the sacristy and see such masterpieces as Tintoretto's folksy hit on the *Marriage at Cana*, where he got his friends to pose and women are in charge of pouring wine out of giant jugs. Titian's ceiling paintings here are also stunning, especially *The Sacrifice of Abraham*, where an angel swoops in to save Abraham's son Isaac, depicted as an adorable three-year-old with Titian-colored hair. Use the mirrors set on the side benches to get the best view.

In a corner are four simple Madonna portraits by Sassoferrato, a Baroque painter who was influenced by Raphael. Though critics call them too sentimental, they win me over.

Santa Maria della Salute: Dorsoduro 1, open daily 9-noon, 3-5:30

❂ Church of Santa Maria del Rosario*

The story goes that in the thirteenth century Saint Dominic had a vision of the BVM directing him to pray the rosary, and so he founded an order that has been devotees of her beads ever since. In the eighteenth century, Venetian Dominicans decided to take over a floundering church that was originated by *I Gesuati* (Poor Followers of Jesus) and build a whole new structure—something impressive to promote their order and praise their Lady of the Rosary. Top architect of the day, Giorgio Massari, designed it in classical style with a swirly Rococo interior. Though the Dominicans renamed the church Santa Maria del Rosario, Venetians never took to the change, and to this day they still call it "dei Gesuati."

Check out the pretty ceiling, where Giovanni Battista Tiepolo, an artist known for dramatic flair, painted Mary handing the rosary to Saint Dominic. On the right as you enter is another Tiepolo: *The Virgin Appearing to Donimican Saints*, Saint Catherine of Siena, Saint Rose of Lima, and Saint Agnes of Montepulciano. On the left is the most honored sculpture in the church: the Madonna of the Rosary.

The Dorsoduro is my favorite neighborhood to stay in when I visit Venice, so I've often found myself at *Chiesa dei Gesuati* for Sunday mass, where I'm surrounded by Venetian families, singing in high spirited celebration.

Church of Santa Maria del Rosario: Fondamenta delle Zattere 918, Dorsoduro, open Monday-Saturday, 10-5, closed Sunday after morning mass

Cannaregio

❖ **Church of Santa Maria dei Miracoli***

This tiny glowing marble treasure chest looks like it should be kept under glass in a museum. If you catch it on a sunny day, it shimmers. It was built with marble left over from San Marco, by Pietro Lombardo, who fitted pink, gray, and butter-yellow stones together to dazzling effect inside and out.

The motivation to build this church came from a portrait of the Madonna that in the fifteenth century was kept in a Cannaregio neighborhood yard. Venetians used to stop and pray to it, and miraculously their prayers were answered. It became so popular that people started to leave money in front of the portrait—enough to fund the building of a church, which became Santa Maria dei Miracoli. In fact, so much money was given that a second story and a convent were added.

The miraculous Madonna portrait now sits at the altar, up a flight of marble steps. The church's gilded ceiling is painted with fifty portraits of saints and prophets, there are pillars carved with mermaids, *putti*, and floral motifs. It all blends seamlessly to create a romantic Renaissance masterpiece. It's no wonder this is the first choice for brides around the world who want to get married in Venice.

Church of Santa Maria dei Miracoli: Campo dei Miracoli, open Monday-Saturday, 10-5

❂ **Church of Madonna dell'Orto**
Along a quiet canal out bursts this Venetian Gothic masterpiece, impressively decorated with statues of the apostles, along with the Archangel Gabriel and BVM flanking the doorway, symbolizing the Annunciation.

Like the dei Miracoli, this church was also inspired by a Madonna artwork. It was a sculpture, chiseled by Giovanni di Santi, originally made for the Santa Maria di Formosa church. Sadly for Giovanni, the church found his work subpar and rejected it, so he dragged it back to his Cannaregio yard.

Then came The Miracle: His wife saw the statue glowing and heard strange sounds coming from it. She blabbed this vision to her neighbors and they began to gather to watch. The reigning bishop, who was against Mary-cult activity (this was 1377, 100 years prior to dei Miracoli), ordered Giovanni to take the statue away from public view, by either bringing it into his house or selling it to another church.

Giovanni jumped on the chance to make some cash and tried to sell the statue to his neighborhood church. In keeping with his bad luck, the church was run by the *Humiliati*—an order of poor penitents who couldn't afford his price of 150 ducats. But coincidentally, the newly formed Scuola of Merchants was headquartered next to the church, and they jumped at the chance to buy it to advertise their success and wealth. The sale was a win for the *Humiliati*, who knew the statue would attract worshippers with donations, which could help pay for finishing the building. In thanks to the Madonna dell'Orto (Madonna of the Orchard), they dropped their Saint Christopher patronage and named the church in her honor. You can see Giovanni's not so pretty Madonna statue in the church's San Mauro chapel.

The church's theatricality is thanks to the prolific, exuberant, sixteenth-century painter Tintoretto (read more about him in the Scuola San Rocco entry). This was his parish church, and he went at it with gusto, painting such glowing scenes as the *Miracle of Saint Agnes* and *the Presentation of the Virgin*.

Church of Madonna dell' Orto: Cannareggio 3512, open daily 10-5, Sunday noon-6

San Marco

❁ Church of Santa Maria del Giglio*

Peek into this tiny gem to see the only Peter Paul Rubens painting in Venice, tucked into a chapel on your right. In classic Rubens style, it's a bare-breasted, voluptuous *Madonna and Child with Young Saint John*.

The name "del Giglio" means "of the Lily," as this flower is often seen held by the angel in Annunciation motifs, such as the altar statue here. The church is also called **Santa Maria Zobenigo**—for the noble family who founded it in the ninth century. It was later glamorized thanks to the patronage of Admiral Barbaro; he's the one to thank for the flamboyant Venetian baroque facade.

Church of Santa Maria del Giglio: Campo Santa Maria Zobenigo, open Monday-Saturday 10-5, closed Sunday

Castello

❁ Church of Santa Maria Formosa

"She was *Formosa* (buxom)," was how a seventh-century bishop described the BVM who came to him in a dream and whispered a simple request: "Build me a church, exactly where I have left a white cloud." The church became one of the first in Venice. It was built of wood, burned, and was replaced with a fifteenth-century Renaissance style design. My favorite spot inside is on the right, where you'll find the *Madonna of Misericordia* triptych (Madonna of Mercy), by Venetian Renaissance painter Bartolomeo Vivarini. The left panel depicts Mary's mother and father, the right Mary's birth. In the center, Vivarini's mastery of color and sculptural technique gives the BVM majesty and passion.

Church of Santa Maria Formosa: Campo Santa Maria Formosa, open Monday-Saturday 10-5, closed Sunday

❧

Golden Day: Visit **dei Miracoli**, enjoy a caffè in the adjoining campo to gawk some more at the church exterior. Have lunch at **Fiaschetteria Toscana,** one of late-great cookbook author Marcella Hazan's favorite Venice restaurants. The dining room is elegant, and the kitchen turns out delicious Venetian classics. It's expensive, but they have a good fixed-price-menu option, great wine list, and the apple tart dessert is out of this world. (Salizada San Giovanni Grisostomo 5719, Cannareggio, 041 528 5281, closed all day Tuesday and Wednesday for lunch)

TIP: * *indicates Chorus Churches. These belong to a group of fifteen churches that charge admission to help pay for the restoration and upkeep of the treasures inside. Admission to all of them is included in your Venice Card, or you can buy a pass separately to visit them: www.chorusvenezia.org*

Madonnas by Titian, Bellini, and Tintoretto

THE MOST SPECTACULAR PAINTING of the Assumption you'll ever see is in the **Frari**. It's an action-packed transcendent scene. The first time I saw it, there was an organ rehearsal going on. May you be so lucky.

It appears in the center of this massive church's altar. Mary dances, flying up to golden heaven, her red robe swirling, arms open to the light, she's lifted on a cloud by twenty-two happy *putti*. Bearded God swoops down, like Batman; an angel by his side, crown a-ready. The earthbound apostles fall all over each other in awe over the miraculous moment, as if a wondrous storm is sweeping through.

The painting caused quite a sensation, like the opening of *Star Wars*, when folks back in 1518 first saw what Titian painted. I imagine he was miffed when the Franciscan friars (whose church it was) gave him flak and waffled about paying him, because they thought his dancing Mary was way too provocative compared to the calm scenes of her levitating on a throne, which was the proper, traditional way to portray her. But soon everybody else declared it revolutionary, Titian became a superstar, and to this day the painting is praised as the best Assumption out there.

Also beautiful is Titian's *Madonna di Ca' Pesaro*. Here he broke the rules again, placing Mary at the side of the painting and putting the Doge who paid for it in the center. Jesus playfully squirms away, tugging at Mary's veil. She was modeled after Titian's wife, who died in childbirth not long after the painting was finished.

Titian's teacher, Giovanni Bellini, painted the delicate, bathed in golden light *Madonna* triptych in the sacristy. You can take a seat here to admire this stunning, serene image of Mary surrounded by serenading angels. The Latin inscription translates to: "*Sure gate of heaven, Lead my mind, Direct my life, May all that I do be committed to thy care.*" And yes, the Bellini that you'll be drinking in Venice, that fabulous prosecco and peach juice mixture, was named in honor of this artist.

Basilica dei Frari: San Polo 3072, a walk from San Toma vaporetto stop, open Monday-Friday 9-6, Saturday and Sunday 1-6, check website for occasional concerts (www.basilicadeifrari.it)

Scuola Grande di San Rocco

Next door, in this grand Renaissance building, is another wonderful painting by Titian. It's an Annunciation, where a red-robed angel dances in to break the surprising news to Virgin Mary that she's pregnant. You'll find it upstairs in this place that centers around the artist Tintoretto, who covered it with over fifty of his paintings, making it his lifelong project.

For a short time, Tintoretto was a student of Titian's, but the older artist kicked him out of his studio, some say because Titian was threatened by Tintoretto's talent. It looks to me more like their styles were so different, probably Titian couldn't stand to have this artist, nicknamed "Il Furioso" around.

Tintoretto's paintings have a folksy exuberance, with massive characters jammed together telling stories of dramatic biblical moments. The first painting of his you'll notice on the left as you enter the Scuola is the most bizarre Annunciation I've ever seen. Typically Mary is in a sacred bedroom, with a lovely garden in the background. But here she's in a broken down home, dropping a cloth from her spinning wheel, bewildered and anxious, as a muscular Angel Gabriel bursts in through the brick wall with tumbling *putti* overhead. In the background, Mary's husband Joseph works in the yard, oblivious to the event. It's quintessential Tintoretto, mixing the Divine with the everyday.

The Great Hall upstairs features wall-to-ceiling Old and New Testament scenes. You can pick up mirrors on side carts to get a better look at all that drama above you.

Though the overall effect of Tintoretto's Scuola borders on too Vegas-like for my taste, it's well worth it to stop by here for those two completely different Annunciations.

Scuola Grande di San Rocco: Campo San Rocco, San Polo, open 9:30-5:30 (www.scuolagrandesanrocco.it)

❧

Golden Day: Visit the **Frari** and **Scuola Grande di San Rocco**, then have lunch at **Antiche Carampane**, my favorite restaurant in Venice. It's a cozy, yet sophisticated place that serves some of the best fish you will have in Venice, along with wonderful pastas and desserts. (Rio Tera de la Carampane—next to Ponte delle Tette, San Polo, 041 524 0165, reservations essential, closed Sunday and Monday, www.antichecarampane.com)

38 Palazzo Mocenigo

FOR ARISTOCRATS, EIGHTEENTH-CENTURY VENICE was one big party. You can get a blast of it by strolling through this extravagant palazzo that belonged to the Mocenigo family, a grand line of soldiers and politicians that boasted seven doges over the centuries of their heyday.

The building was redesigned in the early seventeenth century, just when a devastating plague hit Venice and the glory days of the Republic began to fade. Little by little, Venice lost its power and possessions in the Mediterranean. By the eighteenth century, Venetians' fortunes were dwindling. So folks like the Mocenigo decided to make the most of what was left, indulging in pleasures big time.

Venice became the City of Carnevale, celebrating for six months, from October until Lent. Everyone wore masks and cloaks around the city, so they could gamble and cavort with courtesans anonymously. Piazza San Marco was a playground 24/7, filled with fortune tellers, caged lions, trained monkeys, and from the East, giraffes and rhinoceroses. Tourists poured in from all over Europe, impressed by the elegant style Venetians brought to hedonistic behavior.

The fun even included wives. Women wanted to party too—go dancing, to the theatre, and play in the country villas. And since husbands were often away serving the state, or if they were much older than their second wives, since their firsts had died in childbirth, a new position was added to households: the *cicisbeo*. This was a man servant whose duty it was to escort these wives around.

The *cicisbeo* slipped into a formal arrangement, often part of a marriage contract. Some were gay, others were lovers. Traditionally they lived in a room above the married couple and were on hand for everything from holding the ladies' fans and perfumes during outings to pleasuring her in the boudoir. The husband-wife-*cicisbeo* trio made for perfect marriages. Wives were fawned over by their *cicisbeo* and could play as they pleased, while husbands were free to cavort with courtesans.

The background of all the gaiety was the fantastic Venetian baroque ornamentation that's displayed in the immense salons of the Mocenigo palazzo—curvy, gilded furnishings, Burano lace tablecloths, sculpted woodwork, and Murano glass chandeliers shaped like floral bouquets. Mosaic floors celebrate the Mocenigo coat of arms, and ceiling frescos are magnificent, particularly the *Allegory of Marriage* painted by Jacopo Guarana, to celebrate the wedding of the Doge Alvise IV's nephew to Laura Corner.

The palazzo's unique attraction is that it's also the **Study Center of the History of Fabrics and Costumes**, so rooms come alive with mannequins posed as if at a party, dressed in the formal styles of the day. Ladies silk gowns are in dreamy ivory and jewel tones, with tight low-cut bodices, poofed skirts, embroidered with pearls and gold. Even menswear became feminine—flared brocade jackets decorated with lace, dazzling vests embroidered with colorful flowers, and elaborate cloaks.

A perfume exhibition completes the sensual experience. Watch the short video to see how the eleventh century Byzantium beauty, Teodora Dukas, is to thank for bringing perfume to

Venice when she married a doge. The Venetians disapproved of Teodora's extravagant ways—eating with a napkin and fork—but they did take to her perfume, as it probably was a welcome relief from the canal stench. With Teodora's inspiration, Venice rose to become the greatest importer of fragrance extracts in Europe. A booming perfume and cosmetic market began here in the Renaissance and lasted until 1797, when Napoleon stormed in and France took over the fragrance biz.

Tantalizing rooms in this section of the palazzo celebrate the magic of perfume making—with displays of gorgeous Murano glass bottles, a recreation of an alchemist's lab, and a perfume maker's organ where a master would work, blending varieties of scents. There is even an interactive area where you can sniff around twenty-four containers of essences—from floral to citrus to spicy.

This section was created by Mavive parfums, pro scent makers who have been on the scene for over a hundred years. They also created a "Merchant of Venice" retail line, so you can buy their perfumes that celebrate Venetian tradition in the museum gift shop.

Museo di Palazzo Mocenigo: Santa Croce 1992 at San Stae vaporetto stop, open April-October, 10-5, November-March: 10-4, closed Monday (www.mocenigo.visitmuve.it)

❧

Golden Day: Visit the Palazzo Mocenigo, then have lunch at **La Zucca**, a charming place that's famous for their extraordinary vegetable specialties—you must have the pumpkin flan. (Calle del Tintor, near Riva de Blasio and San Giacomo dell'Orto,

Santa Croce 1762, 041 524 1570, closed Sunday, reservations essential)

TIP: *Palazzo Mocenigo is one of ten Civic Museums included in the Venice City Pass, which is worth buying if you want to experience Venetian treasures. Info: www.veneziaunica.it*

RECOMMENDED READING

A Venetian Affair: A True Tale of Forbidden Love in the 18th Century by Andrea Di Robilant

39 The Peggy Guggenheim Collection

PEGGY GUGGENHEIM WAS ONE OF THE twentieth century's great bon vivants. How fitting that her home base for thirty years was this airy palazzo on the Grand Canal. Today it's filled with a fabulous collection of modern art she acquired, including paintings and sculptures by such masters as Picasso, Kandinsky, de Chirico, and Mondrian.

Peggy's spirit lives on in these surroundings that resonate with the spicy times she and her artist friends had here from 1949 to 1979. You can imagine her stepping off the terrace into her private gondola for her daily ride, which she took religiously at sunset, wearing a flamboyant get-up and those signature butterfly-shaped sunglasses.

Born in New York in 1898, Peggy was the free-spirited rebel of the wealthy Guggenheim family. Her father died in the sinking of the *Titanic* when she was fourteen. When she came of age and inherited her fortune, she took off for Europe and married writer Laurence Vail, who was nicknamed King of the Bohemians. They honeymooned in Capri, lived in Paris, and bopped around the continent, stopping in Venice where her lifelong passion for the place took hold.

By the time she was thirty-nine, Peggy was divorced, her two kids were in boarding school, and as she puts it, "I needed something to do." A friend suggested she open an art gallery.

Even though she knew nothing about modern art, she dove in, with Marcel Duchamp by her side to educate her. She made a vow to buy one painting a day and decided, taking Samuel Beckett's advice, that she would only buy the work of living artists. Duchamp and Beckett were not only friends who guided her along. They were just two of Peggy's myriad line-up of lovers she became famous for throughout her life. When asked in her later years, "How many husbands have you had, Mrs. Guggenheim?" she cracked back: "D'you mean mine or other people's?"

Her first gallery show in New York made a big splash—introducing the world to painters such as Robert Motherwell, Mark Rothko, and Jackson Pollock. It was Peggy's generous patronage of the American avant-garde that helped to bring international recognition to the movement.

"I have never been to a city that has given me the same sense of freedom as Venice," Peggy says in her autobiography. In 1949, when she was fifty-one, she settled there, buying the Palazzo Venier dei Leoni in the Dorsoduro *sestiere*. The eighteenth-century, one-floor building was perfect for her to sunbathe on the roof and display her sculptures in the garden. Little by little, more and more of her home became gallery space, and while she lived there, she opened it to the public a few afternoons a week. She willed the palazzo to her uncle's Solomon R. Guggenheim Foundation, so today it's been expanded and stands as one of the world's most important small museums of contemporary art.

The Peggy vibe throughout the museum is palpable. A fantastic silver headboard designed by Alexander Calder graces what was her bedroom. A pair of paintings by the surrealist Max Ernst feature monstrous half-naked female images, draped in orange capes, interpreted as being inspired by Peggy. She was married to Max from 1942 to 1946. It was a tumultuous relationship, largely because Max was still in love with Leonora Carrington, a surrealist painter whom he'd left behind in France when Peggy helped him to escape the Nazis and come to America.

One of the first sculptures Peggy bought for the villa appears center stage on her terrace: *The Angel of the Citadel* by Marino Marini. This Etruscan-inspired bronze features an ecstatic rider on horseback—so ecstatic he has an enormous hard-on. Peggy loved peeking out from her sitting room to watch visitors' shocked reactions to the statue. And out of respect, because the terrace faced the Venetian prefect's home, she had the figure cast with a removable penis, so when nuns rode by on their way to get the patriarch's blessing, she'd remove it.

Peggy died at eighty-one and her ashes are buried in the museum's garden, alongside those of fourteen beloved Lhasa terriers she kept throughout her Venetian life. Nearby is an olive tree (a gift from Yoko Ono), and sculptures by such artists as Arp and Moore.

Along with the great collection, this place has wonderful docents. In contrast to most Italian museums, where employees typically slump on folding chairs and bark "No photo!" from time to time, here you'll find young, enthusiastic types. They're art students from all over the world on Guggenheim internships, thrilled to be in Venice and delightful to talk to about what Peggy collected. Just as Peggy brought a fresh spirit of adventure to Venice, these docents keep her spark alive.

Peggy Guggenheim Collection: open daily 10-6, closed Tuesday (www.guggenheim-venice.it)

❧

Golden Day: Visit the **museum**, lingering a while in the **caffè** for a drink (hot cocoa on a wintry day is fab) or snack. Enjoy the Dorsoduro neighborhood, with a stop by **Cantinone Già Schiavi** wine bar (Fondamenta Nani 992), and eat at **Ai Gondolieri**, a romantic, old school place for such specialties as *Fegato alla Veneziana*, liver and onions. It's one of the few places in Venice that doesn't serve fish. (Sestiere Dorsoduro 366, 39 348 808 9829, closed Tuesday, www.aigondolieri.it)

TIP: *Speaking of contemporary art, every two years (odd ones), there is the Venice Biennale, an international exhibition featuring artists from all over the world. www.labiennale.org*

RECOMMENDED READING

Out of This Century: The Autobiography of Peggy Guggenheim by Peggy Guggenheim

Art Lover: A Biography of Peggy Guggenheim by Anton Gill

40 Palazzo Fortuny

VENETIANS CALLED THIS PLACE "The House of the Magician." It's where Mariano Fortuny, who became world famous for his outrageously gorgeous fabrics, gowns, and lamps, set up his home and workshop in 1907. There was a woman behind his success: Henriette Negrin, who he met in Paris in 1897, when she was a French widow, a model and a seamstress. She became his muse, collaborator, and wife—after they lived together for twenty-two years. You'll see Fortuny's paintings of Henriette here—some nude, others of her dressed elegantly with her hair swept up, along with photographs of their trips to Greece and Egypt, where Fortuny got lots of inspiration.

In the museum where they once lived and worked together, you enter the world of this eccentric, twentieth-century Renaissance man. Fortuny was born in Granada in 1871, to both a father and grandfather (on his mother's side) who were highly acclaimed painters in Spain. His father died when he was three, so his mother took him to live in Paris, and also traveled about, until they finally settled in Venice, because Fortuny was horribly allergic to horses, and this was the only place around without carriages.

After his early artistic endeavors in painting and photography and success in designing sets and lighting for theater, Fortuny, at thirty-six years old, began his work on printed fabrics here with Henriette. He'd already had an attic studio in the Gothic palazzo and then bought the building that had been cut up into apartments and gutted it, turning it into a free-flowing creative space.

The walls of the first floor's large rectangular room are covered with Fortuny's patterned fabrics, creating a warm, exotic, colorful ambience. His paintings and lamps surround displays of his models for theatre sets, and his gowns that were worn by such illustrious women as Eleanora Duse, Sarah Bernhardt, and Isadora Duncan.

Fortuny broke into the woman's fashion world in 1907 with his Delphos gown, inspired by tunics from ancient Greek statuary. It was simple and finely pleated, in soft, shimmering colors. Women happily tore off their corsets to put on the sensational dress that elegantly draped their bodies. He packaged it rolled up in a hatbox, so it was easy and light for travel.

On the second floor of the museum is Fortuny's library and personal workshop, where you'll get a hit of the practical side of this free-spirited artist. It's packed with volumes of books about artists who came before him, lots of journals where he catalogued designs and colors, his paints and tools. Fortuny's preferred entrance to this palazzo was climbing through the skylight, straight into this workshop.

Depending on what is being exhibited, you may get to see the expansive top floor of the building. The views from here, through the wavy glass windows, are some of the best in Venice: red roofs, church tops, the ever-changing sky...it's marvelous to imagine how he was inspired here.

Fortuny's fabric designs, of intricate swirls, animals, and geometric prints, clearly show his influences from Spain and travels to Greece and farther east. But ultimately, they're completely Venetian, reflecting the cultural melting pot of the city, with rich colors muted by the city's fog, or glistening in gold or silver sunlight. He was called "the magician" because nobody could figure out exactly how he produced these fabrics, and his techniques are still kept secret.

You'll be so tempted to reach out and touch them in the museum, but you can't. For a tactile experience, head to the **Fortuny Showroom** on Giudecca, or one of the **Venetia Studium** stores in Venice, where you can buy a Fortuny-inspired scarf, pillow, purse, or lamp, to keep a little bit of the Venetian magician in your life.

Palazzo Fortuny Museum: Campo San Beneto (San Marco), 10-6, closed Tuesday (www.fortuny.visitmuve.it)

Showroom: Fortuny SPA, Giudecca 805, 041 528 7697 (www.fortuny.com) Call for an appointment and ask to see the newly designed Countess Gozzi gardens out back. The show-room is next to **Hilton Molino Stucky**, which has a great terrace to stop for a cocktail and enjoy the view of the Venice mainland.

Venetia Studium Stores: San Marco 2403, Calle Larga XXII and in Dorsoduro 180/A, near Punta della Dogana (www.venetiastudium.com)

৯৻৻

Golden Day: Visit the **Palazzo Fortuny** and have lunch at the elegant **Acqua Pazza**, serving excellent seafood, cooked in the southern Amalfi Coast style, with Campania wines to match. (Campo Sant'Angelo, San Marco, 041 277 0688, noon-3, 7-11, closed Monday, www.veniceacquapazza.com)

TIP: *If you'd like to see more Venetian textile treasures, head to the Bevilacqua family shops for gorgeous velevets and brocades. (Fondamenta Cononica, San Marco and Campo Santa Maria del Giglio, www.bevilacquatessuti.com)*

41 Taste Venice

VENETIAN CUISINE IS ELEGANT, with exotic touches from its days as a center for trade with the Middle East. You'll enjoy extraordinary fish from the lagoon, along with the Veneto's outstanding wines—from enticing prosecco to rich, deep Amarone.

Traditional Dishes to Order

- **Antipasti:** *Carpaccio* (thinly sliced raw beef), *Bacala mantecato* (creamed salted cod), *folpeti* (baby octopus)
- **Primi:** *Pasta e fagioli* (pasta and beans), *Risi e Bisi* (rice and beans), *Risotto al nero di seppie* (with squid ink), *Bigoli in Salsa* (thick spaghetti with a sauce made from sardines or anchovies), *Polenta e schie* (with small shrimp)
- **Vegetables:** *Fondi di carciofo* (artichoke bottom), *Radicchio alla Trevignana* (radicchio)
- **Secondi:** *Sarde in Saor* (sardines marinated in a sweet/sour mix with onions and raisins), *Fegato alla Veneziana* (calf's liver and onions), *Anatra Ripiena* (stuffed duck), fish according to the season

If you are in Venice in April or November, there are two lagoon specialties, only caught at that time: **Moeche** (soft-shelled crab) and **Canocchie** (mantis shrimp): They are what to order!

* **Dolce:** *Tiramisu, Fritelle* (fried dough sprinkled with powdered sugar), *Buranei* (simple cookies from the island of Burano—"S" shaped or doughnut shaped)

My Favorite Restaurant

* **Antiche Carampane**, Rio Tera delle Carampane, San Polo 1911, 041 524 0165, closed Sunday and Monday, reservations essential (www.antichecarampane.com)
  It's worth going through the challenge to find this place, near the Ponte de Tette (Bridge of Breasts), a spot where working girls once lived in Renaissance days. Now you are welcomed to this cozy, yet sophisticated dining room that serves some of the best fish you will have in Venice, along with wonderful pastas and desserts.

A Few Favorite Caffès

* **Caffè Florian,** Piazza San Marco (www.caffeflorian.com)
  Hands down my favorite caffè on earth, and absolutely worth the splurge. It opened in 1720, making it Italy's oldest caffè, and Casanova enjoyed coming here because it was the only place at the time that admitted women. It's lovely to settle into the red velvet banquettes, and when the evening orchestra starts up, it feels like you're in a dream world.

* **Caffè dei Frari,** Fondamenta dei Frari (San Polo 2564)
  A cozy spot, directly across from the Frari church, that's been around since 1870. It attracts the range from students to local *nonnas,* and many find themselves lingering in the upstairs salon. They serve low-priced salads, panini, and tramezzini

(delicious sandwiches made with soft white bread), along with good coffee, beer on tap, and wine by the glass.

❀ **Caffè del Doge,** Calle dei 5 (Rialto)
You'll find more locals than tourists here, crowding in for what has been called the best coffee in Venice. Choice beans are masterfully roasted, and the company has expanded to a franchise, with outlets in California and Tokyo.

Bakery/Sweet Shop/Caffè

❀ **Marchini Time,** Campo San Luca, (Santa Croce)
Perfectly placed between San Marco and the Rialto, this tiny bakery is jammed with locals elbowing for places at the counters. They serve excellent coffee to enjoy with a range of their goodies—from jam-stuffed cornetti to almond biscotti, artisinal chocolates, and Torta del Doge—a small cake flavored with raisins, pine nuts, and butter that makes a delicious souvenir. The smiling staff is as sweet as their creations.

Gelato

❀ **Il Doge,** south end of Campo Santa Margherita (Dorsoduro)
In a lively location, typically filled with a younger crowd, try the delicious *Crema del Doge*, flavored with bits of orange, along with excellent standards and specialties of the season.

❀ **La Mela Verde,** Fondamenta de l'Osmarin (Castello)
Young, passionate, and handsome gelàto makers—Davide and Johnny—churn out fabulous flavors—Green Apple, *Mela Verde* being the most famous. They also make crepes and gelato-stuffed cakes. I love the location, near the **Church of**

San Zaccaria, where there was once a wealthy Benedictine convent, full of girls from noble families who became famous for their wild behavior. Peek inside to see Bellini's gorgeous Madonna and Child altarpiece.

❀ **Alaska,** Calle Larga dei Bari 1159 (Santa Croce)
Owner Carlo is a fanatic who gets his gelato ingredients fresh from the Rialto market every day and is always churning up flavors of the season, along with great renditions of standards.

Chocolate

❀ **Vizio Virtù,** Calle del Campaniel (off Campo San Toma, San Polo 2898/A)
Award-winning Mariangela Penzo is the master chocolatier of this shop. Her scrumptious artistic creations include chocolate flavored with pumpkin, artfully designed candies, pralines, jams, and even masks made out of chocolate. It's a great place to snuggle into on a chilly Venice day and indulge in hot chocolate, or in warmer months enjoy their rich gelato.

Wine Bars

In the place that does everything differently, here wine bars are called *bacari*, the snacks are called *cicchetti*. A drink of wine is called an *ombra*, which means shade. That's because back in the old days wine sellers in San Marco would move their carts to the *shade* of  the Campanile to keep their wine cool, and workers would take a wine and panini break there. In warmer months, you'll want a *spritz*—sparkling water, prosecco, and Aperol or Campari.

✲ **Cantinone Già Schiavi**, Fondamenta Nani, Dorsoduro
992, closed Sunday
On a quiet canal in the Dorsoduro *sestiere*, across from a
gondola workshop, this family-run nineteenth-century wine
store is where old-time regulars go elbow-to-elbow with
foreigners, spilling out of the tiny place to the San Trovaso
bridge. Inside it's floor to ceiling wine bottles, with a great
selection of local vintages to buy. Prices are low for wines by
the glass, and the cicchetti, made by Mama Gastaldi, is excellent. I had my first *baccala mantecato* (whipped *baccala* on toast)
here decades ago, and have been hooked ever since.

✲ **All' Arco**, Calle Arco, San Polo 436, open 8-2:30,
closed Sunday
A popular spot with the fishermen and sellers of the Rialto
Market, here owners Francesco and Matteo fix up excellent
ciccheti, including great vegetable selections, depending on
the season, such as marinated artichokes or green beans.

✲ **Cantina Do Mori**, Calle dei Do Mori 429 (San Polo),
closed Sunday
Around the corner from All'Arco, you'll find a quieter scene
at the oldest wine bar in Venice, from 1462. It's done up
in dark wood, with copper pots hanging from the ceiling.
Prosecco is served in old-fashioned, curvy-stemmed glasses,
and there's even the traditional wine *sfuso* (table wine) hosed
out from barrels. Cicchetti can be pricey, with choices rang-
ing from marinated artichoke bottoms to delicate tramezzini.

❋ **La Cantina,** Campo San Felice, Cannareggio, closed
Sunday
There is no menu at this wine bar/restaurant, but anyone
looking for great fish (the *crudo* especially, is fantastic) and
a wonderful selection of Veneto wines must come here.
Though service can be hit or miss, the atmosphere is one big
fun Venetian party.

42 Cooking Class with Patrizia

"I'LL MAKE YOU A SPRITZ!" says Chef Patrizia, the moment I enter her apartment. I barely have my coat off when this darling sprite-of-a-signora hands me the classic Venetian refreshment: a sparkling glass of Campari, mixed with prosecco, garnished with an orange slice. Chef Patrizia, her assistant/translator Silvia, and Lisa, another student, toast: *"Cin cin!"* The vibe is set for a happy party/cooking class.

School began earlier that morning, when I met assistant Silvia and Lisa at the Rialto market. This bustling spot by the

famous bridge has been The Venetian Food Shopping Center since 1097. It's a great scene of curious tourists like me and natives, strolling through the fish stalls that glisten with the bounty from the lagoon and beyond— from squirming live crabs, to shrimp, octopus, tiny clams, and sea bream. Next to the fish market are vibrant stands of fruits and vegetables, overflowing with goodies such as bright purple Treviso cabbage and ripe, orange *Kaki*—a variety of persimmon that's a popular dessert fruit.

With our bags full, we wove through narrow *calle*, along canals, over little bridges, and past the massive Santa Maria Formosa church. Along the way, Silvia turns out to be an excellent guide—showing me the top cheese shop near the market ("Casa del Parmigiano—I saw Mario Batali there!"), a good pizza place, ("Cip Ciap—my husband is Neapolitan and he loves this pizza!), and pointing out the variations in the winged lion sculptures found all over Venice: "If the lion is holding an open book in its paw, that means Venice was at peace, and if the book is closed, it was made when the city-state was at war."

Finally we land in front of a palazzo in the Castello *sestiere*, and zigzag up stairs to Patrizia's apartment. Patrizia is in her sixties, but has the energy of an eight-year-old girl, flitting around in a black mini-skirt and vest that's embroidered with flowers, Alpine style. Her airy apartment is decorated with folksy touches: marionettes, framed needlework pieces, and a wood-burning stove. Right off the kitchen is a terrace, where students dine in warmer months, enjoying a lovely view, with the steeple of San Marco in the background.

Patrizia typically designs the menu herself, based on what's in season, but when I booked the class I asked if I could learn to make one of my favorite Venetian specialties: Sarde in Saor. It's a traditional dish of fried sardines marinated in onions, vinegar, and sugar, resulting in an intense, savory flavor. Marinating it for at least a few days is essential to the recipe.

Chef Patrizia pulls out a surprise: a Sarde in Saor she made for me a few days ago, so I could taste her proper rendition, and then shows me another version she's made: Verdure in Saor, where sardines are replaced with sautéed zucchini, potatoes, eggplant, and peppers.

"We make both so you learn, but first we start with my dessert—my invention!" Patrizia says. It's a brilliant mix of mascarpone, sugar, cocoa, and raisins soaked in grappa (the signature liquer of the Veneto region). We set it aside to chill in the refrigerator before the Saor lesson begins.

With four of us women in the kitchen plus Spritz refills, talk inevitably turns to men and amore, along with lots of laughs.

I get busy gutting sardines and chopping onions, as Patrizia stands by and tells me the Sarde in Saor story. The dish originated centuries ago when fishermen would be at sea for weeks at a time and since there was no refrigeration, their wives invented a way of preserving fish so it would last for their husbands' time away from home. In the Renaissance, pine nuts and raisins were added to the recipe, to aid digestion and sweeten the breath.

The kitchen fills with the homey aroma of onions slowly cooking in oil. Patrizia hands me toothpaste to wash my hands, her clever way to take away the fishy sardine smell.

Our work done, we gather at the table set with pretty lace placemats and floral-patterned china. The taste of Patrizia's pre-prepared Sarde in Saor is so much richer and more satisfying than the one I just made. We savor the tasting/learning experience, toasting with Venetian wine. The lunch ends sweetly with Patrizia's dessert invention, then caffè, "corrected," as the Italians say, with a few drops of grappa.

We linger at the table, in a delightful, well-fed haze, as the afternoon light fades.

Cooking with Chef Patrizia: The International Kitchen, a company that offers classes all over Italy (www.theinternationalkitchen.com)

43

Venetian Spa and Hair Salons

For the ultimate spa experience...

Bauer Il Palladio Hotel and Spa

Visiting this dreamy place begins with a private boat ride from the Bauer Palazzo dock, steps away from San Marco. In minutes, you're dropped on Giudecca Island, where you are welcomed to a sixteenth-century masterpiece property designed by the Renaissance superstar Andrea Palladio. The building was once a convent, then a sanctuary for *zitelle*—girls between the ages of twelve and eighteen who had no dowries. They learned lace making here, a craft that kept them from heading out to the canals to join in and earn money in the world's oldest profession.

The sanctuary has been restored to a luxurious hotel and spa, retaining beautiful touches from its past, such as a long marble basin where you can imagine the *zitelle* lined up doing their laundry. Behind the main building is a breathtaking complex of three gardens, each ingeniously landscaped to conjure a different mood. One is English style, with rows of sculpted boxwood hedges, roses, and lavender. Another is graced with a large magnolia tree and fountain, a third features a pergola draped with grape vines where weddings can be held. Gardens are rare in Venice, and guests enjoy lounging amidst the greenery, or enjoying the pretty view from the patio of the *L'Ulivo* restaurant, that specializes in light and savory fare, locally sourced.

The Spa takes up the lower floor of the main building, offering state-of-the-art treatments, such as Reiki, oligo and elitocosmesi facials (to counteract the effects of aging), a Sea Malay massage...with so many choices, I left it up to the experts to plan my treatment.

Angela designed the perfect remedy for a traveler—detoxifying in a humongous bathtub surrounded by floating rose petals, then a reflexology session on my feet, and hot oil hair treatment. The grand finale was an amazing four-handed massage by Angela and her co-angel, Roberta. When all was finished, I sipped a *tisane* in the relaxing room, mesmerized by the sight of San Marco in the distance.

Night had fallen when it was time to go. My two angels, with beatific smiles, escorted me to the dock, where the boat was waiting to take me back to the mainland. The stars twinkled in the night sky. I was glowing and refreshed, ready to fully enjoy every moment of *La Serenissima*.

Bauer Il Palladio Hotel and Spa, Giudecca, 041 520 7022 3869 (www.palladiohotelspa.com)

Hair Salons

Being out on the water in vaporettos or even on a romantic gondola ride can make it a challenge to keep our hair pretty while in *La Serenissima*. Here are two places where you can take a break and get beautified, Venetian style.

- **Stefano and Claudio,** Riva del Vin, San Polo 1098/B, 041 520 1913, open Tuesday-Saturday 9-5 (www.stefanoeclaudiahairdressing.it)
  Get styled or cut by inspired experts, with a fantastic view of the Grand Canal. The salon is state-of-the-art chic, popular with visiting celebrities and brides.

- **Parrucchieri Trolese,** steps from the San Toma vaporetto stop, San Polo 2876, 041 523 1065 (www.parrucchieritrolese.it)
  A team of thirteen signoras is on hand in this lively beauty shop, that's been family run for three generations. Come for an excellent blowout, cut, or color.

44 Craft Classes in Venice

HOW ABOUT SPENDING SOME TIME in one of Venice's dazzling workshops?

Two suggestions:

Mask Making at Tragicomica

 Tragicomica is the finest spot in Venice to pick up traditional masks, and rent hats, ball gowns, and capes for Carnevale. The store is packed with these fantasy-inspiring goodies, and a wonderful place to browse. It's even more fun to get a hands-on experience in the Tragicomica workshop.

The shop's master maskmaker is Gualtiero Dall'Osto, who follows in the footsteps of artists who began dressing up Venetian partiers in the thirteenth century. His creations have been exhibited internationally, and he's designed costumes and set pieces for theaters all over Italy, including La Scala in Milan.

In the 1970s, Dall'Osto was one of a group who fought successfully to bring back the Venice Carnevale, which Mussolini had put an end to in the 1930s. The traditional pre-Lent party began in Venice in the twelfth century. It was named Carnevale from the Latin for *"Farewell meat!"* because the forty days before Easter were days of abstinence.

The three-hour Tragicomica workshop begins with an entertaining demonstration by Dall'Osto's assistant, Alessandra. Putting on masks, she demonstrates how each one has a story behind it, corresponding to a Commedia dell'Arte character or a bit of Venetian history—from the miserly merchant to the witty servant.

Sandy Osceola and her two daughters remember their time in the workshop as the highlight of their vacation. They picked out blank masks to decorate and got to work in the back room, right where expert artisans turn out the pretty things that fill the Tragicomica shop. Sandy chose a Medico della Peste, the Plague Doctor mold. That's the one you've seen in so many photos, with the long beak-shaped nose and tiny eyeholes. It originated in the sixteenth century when doctors would stuff the nose with a sponge soaked in vinegar, so they could move plague victims around and be protected from the disease. Sandy's daughters, Jessica (21) and Marissa (12), went for styles that they decorated with paints and sequins to look as though they were eighteenth-century ladies on their way to a Carnevale ball.

By lunchtime they had three one-of-a-kind souvenirs. Now back at home, those masks bring back great memories of the trip the Osceolas took to celebrate Jessica's graduation from college. Moreover, the masks will always remind them of the entertaining spirit that pervades the unique city of Venice.

Tragicomica: Calle dei Nomboli, off Campo San Toma in San Polo, 041 721102 (www.tragicomica.it)

Mosaic Workshop at Orsoni Studio

You may be so taken by the mosaics that cover the Basilica San Marco that you'll want to find out more about this amazing art. At Orsoni studio you can get a backstage look at the whole process.

Orsoni is hidden behind high walls in the Cannaregio district, off a *fondamenta* that wasn't even on my *Streetwise Venice* map. Since 1888, when the foundry was taken over by Angelo Orsoni, the *smalti* (colored opaque glass) and gold-leaf mosaics that it produces have been used to restore churches, such as the Basilica di San Marco, and shipped off to provide materials for some of the world's most beautiful buildings—from Gaudi's Sagrada Familia church in Barcelona, to the Golden Room in Stockholm where Nobel Prizes are awarded, to buddhas in Bangkok.

Even though what's made here is such a major deal, the place has a low-key, family business vibe. Everybody from the workers to the staff and students seems especially upbeat, I'm guessing because they're surrounded by all this pretty sparkly stuff all day.

I had a chance to see the production facility, where men gathered around a blazing furnace and moved with a riveting choreography, scooping out glowing liquid glass to a rotating metal belt where it solidified in seconds and then cooled, like iridescent pancakes. Next door, women cut these pancakes (called *smalti*) into *tesserae* (small pieces used in mosaic art) that formed what looked like piles of glittering hard candy. Finally, there's the color library: a huge warehouse of rickety wooden shelves stacked floor to ceiling with over two thousand hues of *smalti* to choose from.

The Orsoni Workshop was opened in 2003 by Maestro Lucio Orsoni, the great-grandson of the company's founder and a world-famous mosaic artist. Classes here are small (six students max), so there's lots of individual attention given by instructor/ artist Antonella Gallenda, who's been working by Lucio's side for over thirty years. The school attracts a range of international students, from beginners to those with years of experience. Some simply sign up for three days to add a little cultural zing to their Venetian vacation and make a small mosaic. Others opt for the one- or two-week sessions to learn basics, micro-mosaics, or portraiture.

Many of them, like Connie Giocobbe from Kansas City, who I met while visiting, are return students. "I came here as a beginner three years ago, and now I'm back for my third time," she said. Connie's technique has advanced so much she's gotten commercial commissions for her creations. The class I observed had a fun, focused, creative spirit in the air, with instructor Antonella strolling from student to student offering encourage- ment and suggestions.

"I've made friends from all over the world here," Connie tells me. "A lot of nights after dinner, we'll go back into the workshop with a bottle of wine and cheese, blast a Pavarotti CD, and get to work. Sometimes we're up until three in the morning. It's completely relaxing."

I slept over in **Domus Orsini**, a bed and breakfast in the same building as the workshop, designed by mosaic artisans, where students can stay during the course. In the morning, I had a surprise wake-up call: the foundry workers singing as they started their work day. Happy sounds, pretty colors, beautiful tradition.

Orsoni Studio and Domus Orsoni: For workshop informa- tion, to make an appointment to tour the foundry and gallery, or to book a stay at **Domus Orsoni** (www.orsoni.com)

45 *Active Venetian Adventures*

Row Venice

I'm glad a pic was snapped to prove I didn't dream this up: There

I am, standing on the stern of a boat, oar in hand, rowing in the Venetian lagoon, just like a gondolier.

The boat is called a *batellina coda de gambero*, shrimp's tail, because of its curved shape. You'll see ones just like it in the eighteenth-century paintings of Canaletto. And the light, near dusk, as I stood there and rowed, had that same, soft Canaletto quality.

Row Venice is the organization that offers such an adventure. It was created by a team of women, among them Nan McElroy, an American who fell in love with Venice and now lives near the dock in Cannaregio where we started our lesson. Though she works in Venice as a tour guide and sommelier, it's turning tourists on to the pleasures of traditional boating that she's most enjoying at the moment.

Nan gives a rowing technique demo before we start, but my learning comes more as I go along, and it soon becomes a series of thrills. First gliding along the back waterways, flanked by lines of laundry, boats delivering groceries, getting a backstage look at real Venetian life, with Nan calling out to her neighbors on the bridges and up to their windows as we row by. Then out in the expanse of the lagoon, rocking with the current, feeling like a speck amidst water taxis and fading light. As the sun sets, we row back through the narrow side canals, under tiny bridges, attaching a light to the prow as the first stars begin to pop into the sky.

"This is why I live here," Nan says, as she sees me tilting my head back, taking it in: the quiet swish of the boat, lights flickering on in the palazzos, the moon rising...

Row Venice: Offers lessons all year long. It's great for families, wonderful at sunset, and Nan can also take you on a cicchetti row, from *bacaro* to *bacaro*. (www.rowvenice.org)

Biking on Sant' Erasmo
(The Secret Garden of Venice)

For a break from the canals, vaporetto over to Sant'Erasmo, an island that lies between Burano and Murano. It's covered with vegetable gardens and orchards that have supplied Venice markets for centuries, and since the soil has a high salt content, the vegetables are especially delicious. If you get there in June, lucky you: there will be fields of purple artichokes in bloom.

The bike loop around the island is a flat three and a half miles, and you may want to join Venetian families at the tiny beach for a swim—this is where the locals come to escape the Lido crowds.

Bike rentals: Lato Azzurro, Via dei Forti 13, 041 523 0642 (www.latoazzurro.it)

꣠

Golden Day: Take Vaporetto 13 to the Capannone stop at Sant'Erasmo, about a thirty-minute ride. Take a bike ride, then eat at **Ristorante Ca'Vignotto**. It's a treasure of a family-run restaurant, the only one on the island, beloved by locals, where you can enjoy freshly picked fruit and vegetables. (Via Forti, 71 041 244 4000, lunch Tuesday-Sunday, dinner Thursday-Saturday, reservations essential, www.vignotto.com)

46 Shopping in Venice

THE SHOPPING SCENE IN VENICE reflects its magical essence. Glass making, lace making, and mask making are traditional crafts that have flourished here since Renaissance days. That said, lots of what you'll see for sale is made in China. If you want the real thing, it's worth seeking out authentic shops and spending your euros for a lasting treasure.

Here's a selection of some of La Serenissima's most beautiful places to browse and buy:

Glass Shopping on Murano

Glass making came to Venice in the Middle Ages, through traders from the Middle East. By the thirteenth century, to prevent fires from flaring up on the mainland, factories were moved to the nearby island of Murano, where you will find them still thriving today.

A visit to Murano makes for a fun trip. From the Fondamente Nove, it's a ten-minute vaporetto ride.

Stop by the **Museo del Vetro** (Glass Museum) for stunning displays of glass through the ages—from first-century Persian pieces to wild twentieth-century creations. This is also where you can sign up to see the awesome art of glassblowing in action—check the website for times.

It's best to visit the island in the morning, before throngs of tourists arrive, who've been lured by offers of free trips to factories. Beware that these free trips, offered by many hotels, typically begin with impressive artisan demonstrations and then turn into hard sells in the showrooms.

And do stop in at Murano's Santa Maria church—the **Basilica Santa Maria e Donato**, a tenth-century Byzantine masterpiece, one of the oldest churches in Venice. Legend says it was built by order of Emperor Otto, to thank the BVM for saving his ship in a storm.

Museo del Vetro: Fondamenta Marco Giustinian 8, open daily 10-5 (www.museovetro.visitmuve.it)

Some Favorite Murano Shops

* **Ercole Moretti,** Fondamenta Navagero 42
  (www.ercolemoretti.it)
  This prestigious institution has been family run since 1911 and produces gorgeous *millefiori*, thousand flower pieces, whereby glass is infused with colorful patterns. A great stop for beads and decorative plates.

* **Marina e Susanna Sent,** Fondamenta Serenella 20, also in Venice, on Campo San Vio 669, Dorsoduro
  (www.marinaesusannasent.com)
  These sisters bring chic modern style and rich colors to glass making, offering beautiful jewelry and tableware.

* **Murano Collezioni**, Fondamenta Manin 1c, (near Murano Colonna vaporetto stop, www.muranocollezioni.com)

Famed glass makers Carlo Moretti and Venini are showcased beautifully in this shop where you can buy their products at discounted prices.

TIP: *To ensure you're getting real Murano glass, look for the Marchio del Cetro Artistico di Murano stamp. This means it has passed quality control inspections, and was made based on original Muranese tradition.*

Lace Shopping in Burano

The island of Burano has been world famous for lace making since the 1500s. The Venetian legend goes that it started when a man who was heading off to sea gave his beloved an intricate piece of seaweed. Pining for him, she took out her needle and copied the design. The more practical story is that these island women were experts at mending their husband's fishing nets, so when lace making came along, they took to it naturally.

Now Burano, a twenty-five minute vaporetto ride from Venice, is covered in lace shops. Stop by the **Museo del Merletto** (Lace Museum) to start your shopping expedition. There's a great video about the history of lace making and elegant displays. Best of all, there are senior citizen *signoras* working there who have been making lace all their lives. The star of them is Emma Vidal, a 97-year-old spunky type, who makes lace without wearing glasses. "The young people don't do this anymore," she grumbled, when I sat next to her, marveling over her quick stitching technique. "All they want to do is dance in the *discoteca!*"

Museo del Merletto, Piazza Baldassare Galuppi 187, open April-October, 10-6, November-March, 10-5, closed Mondays (www.museomerletto.visitmuve.it)

TIP: *The lace making signoras take a lunch break, so stop by between 10 and noon or 2–3:30 to see them.*

Lace Shops in Burano

* **Merletti d'Arte Martina**, Via San Mauro 308 (www.martinavidal.com)
  Come here for lace blouses in beautiful colors and stylish designs, and a wonderful selection of table and bed linens. There is also an attached museum of antique lace. It's close to the vaporetto landing, and their back garden is a pleasant place to enjoy a caffè and those special Buranesi cookies.

* **Emilia Burano,** Piazza Galuppi 205 (www.emiliaburano.it)
  Gorgeous bed and bath linens in this ultra-elegant shop.

In Venice

Masks

* **Tragicomica:** Calle dei Nomboli, off Campo San Toma in San Polo, 041 721102 (www.tragicomica.it)
  A floor-to-ceiling extravaganza of authentic Venetian masks. They also offer mask-making workshops that immerse you in this beautiful artisan tradition.

Jewelry

* **Venetian Dreams,** Calle della Mandola San Marco 3805/a, closed Tuesdays (www.venetiandreams.altervista.org)
  Marisa Convento's welcoming shop is filled with her beautiful and imaginatively designed glass jewelry, along with

beaded purses and slippers. In addition, she loves to meet travelers and share her knowledge and passion for Venice—so you may also get museum and restaurant recommendations from this *Signora Congeniality* of Venice shopkeepers.

* **Gloria Astolfo**, Calle Frezzeria 1581, San Marco
Gloria's jewelry blends a playful and glamorous style, with vibrant pins, bracelets, and necklaces.

* **Esperienze Visman**, Calle Larga San Marco 473/B
(www.esperienzevenezia.com)
Sara Visman, whose ancestors were Murano glassmakers, brings a modern, bold twist to her jewelry designs.

Paper

* **Il Pavone**, Calle Venier dei Leoni 721, Dorsoduro
Here rich colors are blended as brilliantly as those on a *Pavone's* (peacock's) tail, then hand stamped on to paper. You can buy sheets suitable for framing, sheets of paper stamped with gold-flecked geometric or floral patterns, picture frames, neckties, journals, and stationery.

* **Paolo Olbi**, Ponte di Ca Foscari 3653, Dorsoduro
Paolo is a true Venetian artisan who makes such classic, beautiful things as journals covered with intricately hand-tooled leather, Byzantine-patterned paper, and stationery decorated with etchings of Venetian landmarks.

Leather

❋ **Raggio Veneziano**, Campo San Stefano, San Marco 2953
(www.raggioveneziano.com)
Anna Maria Urbani and her husband get the finest leather
from Tuscany to make purses here, which range from chic
cocktail designs to handsome portfolios for men. I love the
latest lines that have sleek outer pockets to slip in your tablet
or e-reader.

Gloves

❋ **Fanny**, Calle dei Saoneri 27/33,
Campo San Polo
Here you'll find top quality leather gloves in a
range of styles—from polka-dot to fur lined, in
every color imaginable. Snatch up a pair to take the Venice
chill away.

Shoes

❋ **Giovanna Zanella Atelier**, 5641 Calle Caminati
(Castello)
Giovanna was a student of the famous, eccentric Venetian
shoemaker, Rolando Segalin. Her creations show his influence—including wacky styles of curved pointed shoes and
ones that look like gondolas. But she's branched out to
include designs that you would wear more often and can
custom-design shoes for you. You may just want to snatch up
what's on the shelves of her adorable boutique—from sneakers to evening wear, and even hats and dresses.

Eye Glasses

❀ **Ottica Carraro**, Calle della Mandola, San Marco 3706
(www.otticacarraro.it)
Come for unique, custom-designed eyewear—from classic
to vintage to funky, in great colors and patterns, reasonably priced.

Perfume

❀ **The Merchant of Venice**, Campo San Fantin, near La Fenice
The esteemed Venetian Mavive perfume company created
this line to pay homage to the Renaissance days when Venice
was famous for its perfume laboratories. The shop is in a
beautiful centuries-old pharmacy, where you can have your
perfume custom-designed by scent specialists.

Clothes, and More

❀ **Banco Lotto No. 10,** Salizada da Sant' Antonin 3478/a
This non-profit boutique carries the creations of the *Casa
di Reclusione Femmnile* (women's prison of Giudecca), who have
been trained to become excellent tailors, making clothes and
accessories, using gorgeous fabrics. The prices are surprisingly low for the high quality, and all profits go to support
the education of the prisoners.

❀ **Venetia Studium Stores**
San Marco 2403, Calle Larga XXII and in Dorsoduro
180/A, near Punta della Dogana (www.venetiastudium.com)
Both shops are stocked with exquisite Fortuny-inspired
lamps, pillows, tablerunners, purses, and scarves—all exclu-
sively made in Venice.

Books

❋ **Wellington Books,** Calle della Mandola, San Marco
(www.wellingtonvenice.blogspot.com)
This recently opened, welcoming shop carries on the great
tradition of the connection between Venice and the English
literary world. It's well stocked with English-language titles
and has a good selection of children's books.

🙶🙶

Golden Day: Vaporetto to Burano and enjoy wandering amidst
the colorful homes along the canals and lace shops, making a
stop at Museo del Merletto to watch the lacemaking *signore* in
action. Have lunch at **Trattoria al Gatto Nero**, for charming
service and great seafood, prepared with risotto, grilled, or
fried. (Fondamenta Giudecca 88, 041 730 120, closed Monday,
www.gattonero.com)

Music in Venice

VENICE HAS LONG BEEN PRAISED as a grand place for music. In its eighteenth-century party heyday, there were seventeen opera houses here, filled to the rafters with a mix of courtesans, merchants, and noblemen.

Remaining beauties of those days are:

* **La Fenice**, one of the most famous opera houses in the world. *Fenice* means phoenix—the mythological bird that rose from the ashes—as the theatre was built in 1792 over another that had burned. The name may have cast a spell on this place, as there were devastating fires again in 1836 and in 1996 that destroyed it. Each time the theatre was rebuilt, with the recent 90 million euro job completed in 2003, restoring the treasure to its original splendor. Along with opera, symphony concerts are performed here throughout the year (www.teatrolafenice.it).

* **Teatro Malibran**, from 1678, is another gorgeous venue for opera and classical music. It was named in honor of the soprano Maria Malibran, who found the theatre in horrible condition when she came here to sing in 1835, so she kindly offered her salary to use to repair the building. (www.teatrolafenice.it)

❋ **Teatro Goldoni** was named in honor of the Venetian playwright Carlo Goldoni, and his Commedia dell'Arte plays are performed here, as well as children's shows, dance, concerts, and contemporary plays (www.teatrostabileveneto.it).

Chamber Music

Venice reveres Vivaldi, that romantic baroque musician of *Four Seasons* (*Quattro Stagioni*) fame, who was born here in 1678. He was a revolutionary composer, boldly bringing emotion to the violin and its sister string instruments—from heights of joy to depths of melancholy. His ornate music matches the Venetian spirit.

All over Venice you'll see posters for chamber ensemble performances where Vivaldi is the headliner. And there will often be other greats such as Corelli, Rossini, and Mozart on the bill. You'll also be approached by beaming costumed folks who are putting on Vivaldi shows. To put it as nicely as possible, the costumed folks are *not* who I mean when I'm talking great Vivaldi in Venice, so don't confuse them with the authentic chamber ensembles.

Tickets are easy to get online, at tourist kiosks, or through your hotel; I've also done fine off-season just showing up right before the concert. Performance nights vary, and most starting times are 8:30ish.

❋ **Interpreti Veneziani**—Chiesa San Vidal, San Marco (www.interpretivenziani.com)
The very best! An exuberant ensemble that's received critical raves internationally since they came onto the scene in 1987. The seventeenth-century church setting is enriched with paintings from Carpaccio and other Venetian masters.

❀ **Ensemble Antonio Vivaldi**—Chiesa di San Giacometto, Rialto (www.ensembleantoniovivaldi.com)
The cherry red interior of one of Venice's oldest churches makes for an especially romantic experience. This is also an exceptionally well-heated venue, perfect for a chilly night.

❀ **Collegium Ducale**—Chiesa di Santa Maria Formosa (Rialto) or Palazzo delle Prigioni, San Marco (www.collegiumducale.com)
This excellent seven-piece ensemble presents programs of Baroque music and concerts of soloists singing arias in two locations, including a building that was once added on to the Doge's Palace to be used as prisoners' cells.

❀ **Musica a Palazzo,** Palazzo Barbarigo Minotto, Fondamenta Duodo o Barbarigo (San Marco, Giglio Vaparetto stop), 340 9717272 (www.musicapalazzo.com)
In the splendid setting of this opulent palace, you're immersed in the passion of classic operas performed by a stellar ensemble.

Jazz

❀ **Venice Jazz Club,** Ponte dei Punghi, San Barnaba (near Ca Rezzonico vaporetto stop), 340 150 4985, closed Thursday and Sunday (www.venicejazzclub.com)
There's a great house jazz band in residence at this welcoming spot that plays a mix of standards, Latin, and blues, with quality guest musicians joining in. Twenty euros gets you your first drink and a table for the evening. Snacks are served before the shows start at 9 P.M.

Also

* **Caffè Florian,** Piazza San Marco (www.caffeflorian.com)
  It's worth the splurge to settle in with a cocktail at this extraordinary caffè from 1720 and pay the six-euro surcharge when the orchestra is playing. This will be an evening for the memory books.

* **Venice Biennale**
  Every two years, the odd ones, Venice hosts an international exhibition of contemporary artists, which also includes film and performance events. (www.labiennale.org)

Venice musical events: www.musicinvenice.com

Side Trips
from Venice

48 The Scrovegni Chapel in Padua

IT'S TOUGH TO PULL AWAY FROM VENICE, but a half-hour train ride will bring you to this splendid fourteenth-century chapel, dedicated to Mary and frescoed by Giotto, who inspired all the Renaissance greats. It was built over ruins of a Roman arena, which is why its real name is the **Church of the Madonna dell'Arena**. But it's better known as the **Scrovegni Chapel**, because it was originally a part of their family villa.

The inspiration to call in Giotto to fresco this place came from Enrico Scrovegni, who was desperate to not burn in hell. His father, Reginaldo, was a scumbag money lender—the embodiment of the worst credit card company you can imagine, who charged ridiculously high interest rates and awful late fees. Reginaldo was so despised that the church denied him a burial. Dante put him in the Seventh Circle of Hell, where he was doomed to sit on hot sand with his head bent while Florentines shouted in his ears for eternity.

Enrico, a wealthy merchant and banker, wasn't so different from his father, so to atone for Reginaldo's sins, save his soul and his family's, he went overboard and called in the best painter of the day to work on the church adjoining his home: Giotto.

You'll walk in to be wowed by the intense blue of Giotto's curved star-studded ceiling that tops thirty-eight frescos, all backed by that heavenly blue, which narrate the life of Mary and then Christ.

Giotto broke the mold of the stiff Middle Ages, bringing emotion to these figures, which in 1306 was as radical as adding special effects to a movie. There's an innocent beauty to every panel. Characters plead, embrace, conspire and lament as angels sweep in like comets.

Here, sort of like how Ron Howard took the *Da Vinci Code* and made it into a movie, Giotto took *The Golden Legend*, a bestselling book of his day, and made a medieval graphic novel with Mary in the lead. *The Golden Legend*, written by a friar, told imaginative stories of Christianity's major players. Folks back then loved relating to holy people in a contemporary way for the first time.

Since you probably haven't read the book, the images need some explanation. Giotto's scenes play out in three tiers, beginning at the top left corner to "establish the conflict," as Hollywood script analysts would say. Joachim, Mary's father, gets thrown out of the temple because after twenty years of marriage, he and his wife Ann are still childless. What follows is Joachim retreating to his fields in despair, sacrificing a goat to lift the barren curse. Meanwhile home-alone Ann receives the news from an angel that she's finally pregnant. The couple rejoices, Mary is born and taken at three years old to the temple.

In the eighth fresco you'll see men lined up with sticks in their hands, for the *The Presentation of the Rods*, which would have given Freud a phallic field day. The story goes that when Mary was fourteen and marriage-ready, the high priest called in every bachelor in town to lay their rod on the altar, and whoever had one that flowered could marry Mary. The guy standing to the side with a beard is Joseph, who figured he was too old to marry a fourteen-year-old, so he doesn't even enter the rod contest. In the next shot, the high priest has convinced him to add his rod, and all the men are huddled and waiting. What follows is *The Betrothal of Mary and Joseph*, with Joseph proudly holding a rod with a blossoming lily, the symbol of Mary. Joseph's miffed contenders stand to the side, one of them breaking a rod over his knee as if to say, "Drat! I wanted to marry Mary!"

On the wall opposite Mary's Annunciation is the *Last Judgment*, said to be painted by Giotto's assistants, because it doesn't have the elegance of the master. Amidst the fires of hell is Reginaldo Scrovegni holding up a model of the chapel to the Madonna in a "Please forgive me! Look at this pretty chapel I made for you!" gesture.

It's good to visit the chapel knowing these stories because you'll only have fifteen minutes inside to view the frescos. The place has been restored and a sterilized, climate-controlled environment created to preserve the artwork. Your visit begins in an antechamber where you view a short film about the chapel before you're escorted in for your limited time with the masterpiece.

Scrovegni Chapel: Piazza Eremitani 8, Daily 9-7. Reservations are a must, so book ahead through the website. That said, I did visit one November weekday without reserving, got a ticket for an hour later, and had pleasant waiting time strolling through the nearby Padua market. (www.cappelladegliscrovegni.it)

How to get there: Trains from Venice leave often, and it takes about a half hour. (www.trenitalia.it)

⁂

Golden Day: Visit the **Scrovegni Chapel**, lunch at **Osteria L'Anfora** (Via del Soncin 13, 496 56629), an old-school trattoria/wine bar for great seafood, and then have your caffè at the classic (since 1831) **Caffè Pedrocchi** (Via VIII Febbraio 15).

TIP: *Check the website, as periodically they offer extended hours for visits at night.*

49 Villa Valmarana Ai Nani in Vicenza

SPRINKLED OVER THE VENETIAN PLAIN are beautiful villas from the sixteenth to the eighteenth centuries. They're the jewels of superstar Renaissance architect Andrea Palladio and his followers, which recall the symmetry and grace of Greek and Roman temples.

You can visit some of them pleasantly from Venice or Padua by taking a boat ride down the Brenta Canal, which stops at the waterway entrances to the villas and a restaurant for lunch. That's a Golden Day right there.

But to get the full Palladio hit, go to the town of **Vicenza**. This is where Palladio was born, and it's packed with his treasures, including the not-to-be-missed **Teatro Olimpico**.

A walk or short bus ride away from Vicenza's historic center takes you to Palladio's famous **Villa Rotonda**, and farther along a favorite of mine: the **Villa Valmarana ai Nani**. "*Nani*" means dwarves, and the name originated with this legend:

Once upon a time, a couple who lived in this villa gave birth to a daughter, who was a beautiful dwarf. Loving their child dearly, they wanted to protect her from feeling different, so they hired dwarf servants and kept her secluded in the villa and walled garden. For many years she was clueless and content, but when she was fifteen, she got curious about what was going on in the outside world. When her dwarf servants were sleeping, she climbed the stone wall, and up rode a handsome fellow on horseback. It was love at first sight for the dwarf-girl, but when she reached out to ride away with him into the sunset, for the first time she realized, "Oh no! I'm a dwarf!" Horrified, she hurled herself off the wall to her death. The servant dwarves heard her cries, woke up, and ran to find her. When they saw their dead mistress, they froze in grief.

That's why you'll see statues of seventeen *nani* atop the villa walls. They're all inspired by Venetian Commedia dell'Arte characters—such as the Doctor, the King, the Knight, and the Turk. When Giustino Valmarana, a theater fan, moved here in 1720, he incorporated the *nani* story as part of his redesign.

The legend probably originated in the seventeenth century, when dwarves were popular characters in royal courts. They were perfect playmates for children, entertaining, and considered good luck tokens. Many were the result of inbreeding, and they were treated like pets, often given away by their mothers, as they weren't considered part of the "real" family and wouldn't be inheriting anything. Cruel, but true.

Once you're past the *nani* and inside the walls, things get elegant: lovely gardens surround a *foresteria* (former farm-laborer's place) and butter-yellow *palazzina*. Inside the little palazzo is where superstar painter Giambattista Tiepolo created some of the most stunning works of his career in the eighteenth century.

Tiepolo was a Venetian master of Rococo, who frescoed this place with theatrical gusto, finishing the *palazzina* interior in only four months. Using a dreamy pastel palate, he created breathtaking scenes from classical myths and legends.

When you enter, you're hit with his *Sacrifice of Iphigenia*, which packs the power of an opera climax. Center stage sits the Greek warrior Agamemnon, pleading to the heavens for mercy as he holds a knife to his daughter Iphigenia's chest. The story goes that Agamemnon ticked off the goddess Diana by bragging that he was a better hunter than she was. To punish him, she silenced the winds, screwing up his fleet. A prophet appeared to Agamemnon and said he'd have to sacrifice his daughter to lift Diana's curse. In Tiepolo's unusual happy-ending version of the story, Diana (on the ceiling) has a change of heart and flies in to substitute a sacrificial deer for Iphigenia. On the surrounding side panels, Tiepolo painted new winds blowing through.

Action-packed love scenes fill the adjoining rooms. There are images from "Orlando Furioso," a Renaissance epic poem, where the gorgeous maiden Angelica makes Orlando absolutely *furioso*, because she can't help but attract the attentions of other men.

In the Foresteria, which was a guesthouse, there's one final Tiepolo masterpiece in the Olympus Room, where Venus is paired with her boyfriend Mars and Diana with Apollo.

The rest of the Foresteria was frescoed by Tiepolo's son, Giandomenico, who moved on to realism and painted images from eighteenth-century life. There are scenes of peasants in the countryside, wealthy folks partying, a carnival—with both a monkey and an African servant serving chocolate!

Framed photographs of the Valmaranas, who still live here, are scattered about. One of their family's twentieth-century heroines was Amalia, who was a mover and shaker in the Italian women's movement after World War II. She helped to found the Catholic Centro Italiano Femminile, an organization that got women involved in the reconstruction of Italy, defending women's rights and helping them get health care.

There's a special charm to this small (for a villa) place that's been in the same family for over three hundred years. The comical statues, colorful garden, sweeping frescos, and family photos blend with its exquisite design to make magic.

Villa Valmarana: open throughout the year, closed Mondays, but different days and times depending on the season. Check www.villavalmarana.com for up-to-date hours and prices.

How to get there: Trains from Venice leave often and take about 45 minutes. (www.trenitalia.it) Or rent a car, so you can explore the outskirts. (www.autoeurope.com)

☙

Golden Day: Visit the **Villa** and enjoy Palladio's masterpieces in Vicenza. For dinner, take a fifteen-minute drive to **Caldogno** and eat at **Trattoria Molin Vecio** (Via Giaroni 116, 0444 585 168, closed Tuesday, www.molinvecio.it). It's built around a mill from 1520, surrounded by a lovely landscape and huge herb garden. Sleep at **Hotel Campo Marzio** (www.hotelcampomarzio.com), a boutique hotel close to the historic center.

TOURS

Boat tours of Italian villas are available from Venice or Padua at www.battellidelbrenta.it or www.ilburchiello.it.

50 *Asolo*

THE APPROACH TO ASOLO (pronounced AHH-zow-low), up a curvy
road through a forest, is absolutely fairytale-ish. It leads you to
an idyllic postage-stamp-sized historic center: Happy locals sitting on the terrace of the **Caffè Centrale**, a fountain, bell tower,
two-story stone buildings bedecked with colorful flower boxes,
a medieval castle perched in the near distance. As you explore,
it immediately lives up to its nickname: "City of One Hundred
Horizons"—you can't walk two minutes without finding yourself
gasping over a stunning view of vineyards and olive groves below
you, with snow-capped mountains in the distance.

The strongest Asolo attraction for me is that it has been
enriched through history by three extraordinary women: a
queen, an actress, and an adventurous travel writer. Adding
to that are feminine spiritual touches—a tiny church honoring Saint Anne (mother of Mary), another dedicated to Saint
Catherine of Alexandria, and a central cathedral dedicated to
the BVM of the Assumption. All this is packed into an area that
could easily be scoped out in an hour. But Asolo is a place that
lures you to linger. It's a perfect complement to the labyrinth
of Venice, as it's impossible to get lost in the quiet, pedestri-
an-friendly vias of the village.

Starting at the Cathedral, you'll find ten BVM paintings and
sculptures. The most bizarre is a fifteenth-century Assumption

panel by Lorenzo Lotto. Here Mary is not the pretty BVM we are accustomed to. In fact she is shockingly elderly. Why? She was modeled after the artist's patron, **Caterina Cornaro, Extraordinary Woman Number One**, the Ex-Queen of Cyprus, who famously reigned in Asolo from 1489 to 1509.

The story goes that in the fifteenth century, Venice very much wanted control of Cyprus, as the island was perfectly positioned to control Mediterranean trade routes. Rather than fight, the Venetians offered Caterina Cornaro, the fourteen-year-old daughter of a noble family, to the King of Cyprus, James II. James accepted, so Caterina was married off, but didn't actually meet him until four years later when she arrived in Cyprus for a face-to-face wedding. One year later, James died, leaving pregnant Caterina to rule. She gave birth to a boy who mysteriously died before his first birthday. The Venetians got nervous about Caterina holding power without an heir, fearing she'd betray them and turn over the reins to the Neapolitans or the Cypriots. So they offered her to gracefully abdicate: *"Honey, how about leaving Cyprus and becoming the Lady of Asolo (that wealthy wool factory center north of Venice), in that beautiful area where we all go to summer? You'll have a castle, a good allowance, a court, soldiers, fresh air.... Just give us Cyprus!"*

Caterina agreed and arrived in Asolo with much pageantry, and great stories for all about her reign on the exotic island of Cyprus. Over her twenty-year stint, she turned the place into an artistic center, inviting such masters to her court as Lotto (painter of that Assumption) and the poet Bembo (author of Gli Asolani). Even the first lady of the Renaissance, Isabella d'Este, came from her palace in Mantua to pay Caterina a visit.

Asolo's attraction as an artsy place stuck from the days of Caterina's reign. In the nineteenth century, the actress **Eleonora Duse, aka The Divine Duse, Extraordinary Woman Number**

Two, found it perfect for a getaway from the limelight. This Italian legendary beauty was born in Piedmont to actor-parents,  joined the family business, then burst forth with a whole new approach to the art of acting. She threw away the poses and oratorical style of the day and became the first modern actress— mining emotional truths within to create performances that stunned audiences and inspired playwrights from Shaw to Chekhov to Ibsen. During breaks, Duse would stay with friends in Asolo, and finally decided to build a villa here. Unfortunately, she never had the chance to live in it, dying at the age of sixty-six in Pittsburgh during an American tour. Still, her beauteous image is honored all over Asolo—with paintings and photos in restaurants and shops, and a theatre named in her honor. It's also a kick to see the Duse display in the museum, which includes personal goodies such as the shawl she wore in *A Doll's House* and her knitting needles from *Ghosts*.

Extraordinary Woman Number Three is Freya Stark, whose villa you will pass as you drive into Asolo. Freya was British, a revolutionary travel writer, photographer, Arabist, and explorer—famous for her adventures in the Middle East. She had fallen in love with Asolo as a child in the early 1900s when her parents took her there to stay with their friend, the poet Pen Browning. Pen's father Robert had bought a villa in Asolo after his wife, Elizabeth Barrett died. (Read more about that in the Casa Guidi-Florence chapter.)

Following decades of adventures, Freya chose to settle down in her beloved Asolo. She died here in 1993, so you can still meet locals who knew her. Today you can tour the exotic garden she kept in the back of her villa, where there are also ruins of a Roman amphitheatre.

A lovely walk from the cathedral through the piazza leads you to the **Church of Saint Caterina**, where you can admire fourteenth-century frescos. Then you'll pass the door of Duse's villa, Villa Cipriani where Queen Elizabeth stayed when she came to visit her friend Freya, and finally you'll arrive at Saint Anne's church cemetery. It's set into a hillside, all neat white stones adorned with flowers. Signs make it easy to find the most sought after graves: Freya Stark's and Eleanora Duse's, dramatically facing Monte Grappa in the distance.

You can stand there in reverent silence for a moment, believing it must have been Asolo that inspired one of the Divine Duse's most beloved quotes:

"If the sight of the blue skies fills you with joy, if a blade of grass springing up in the fields has power to move you, if the simple things of nature have a message that you understand, rejoice, for your soul is alive..."

Asolo Tourist Info: www.asolo.it, www.bellasolo.it, www.marcatreviso.it

How to get there: Asolo is about an hour's drive north of Venice. To rent a car, www.autoeurope.com.

Public transportation from Venice involves a few transfers. Take the train to Montebelluna (a half hour), then a taxi. Or from Montebelluna take a bus, then shuttle to the town center.

❧

Golden Day: Start at **Caffè Centrale**, then explore shops, the museum, and the cathedral, before a walk to Saint Anne's cemetery. Have lunch at a picnic table outside **Corte dei Rei**, enjoying their specialty porchetta, or plates of salumi and mountain cheeses, and mulled wine in fall and winter. Or go to **Antica Osteria al Bacaro** (via R. Browning 165 0423 55150) a popular spot for wine and snacks, where the *bigoli* (thick housemade spaghetti) with radicchio is excellent. Continue the adventure with an easy hike up to **La Rocca**, to explore the remains of a medieval castle and enjoy stunning views of the Veneto plain.

TIP: *Since museums and restaurants have closing days Monday–Wednesday, it's best to plan your trip accordingly.*

Stay

* **Hotel Duse** (www.hotelduse.com)
  A perfectly located three-star in the center, where you'll love meeting owner Alessandro and his mother Gabriella who will thrill you with stories of the glamorous days of Asolo.

* **Hotel Villa Cipriani** (www.villacipriani.it)
  A romantic, luxurious option, with a gorgeous landscaped garden and sophisticated dining room.

* **Villa Freya Stark's Garden** (www.bellasolo.it)
  Open the first three Saturday mornings of the month, and by appointment.

Shopping

❋ **Monthly Antique Market**
On the second Saturday of every month and following Sunday, this market takes over the historic center of town.

Women-Owned Shops

❋ **Il Pozzo Antichita,** Via Roma 58, closed Tuesday
Great selection of antique jewelry.

❋ **Ceramiche La Bot,** Via Robert Browning 166
(www.ceramichelabot.it)
Hand-painted ceramics with an open workshop.

❋ **Scuola Asolana di Antico Ricamo**, Via Canova 333
(www.scuolaasolanaanticoricamo.it)
Founded by Pen Browning (son of poet Robert) in 1891, it's now a charming spot to see delicate Asolian style embroidery, made by Francesca, who you can watch at work in the upstairs studio.

Appendix 1
Tips for Italian Travel

1. **Lie about when you're leaving and returning.** Tell yourself and those in your world you'll be away the day before and the day after whatever it says on your airplane ticket. It's not really lying. Mentally you're in Italy those pre- and post-travel days. This helps me to not leave packing until the last minute, and spares those around me from being with getting-on-the-plane-to-Italy-obsessed Suz. The day after you return, you'll be on an Italy high, unpacking and will get no sympathy with your "I'm jet-lagged, just got back from Italy" spiel. Consider these border days gifts to yourself, to ease in and out of the journey. If you do tell one person your *real* return date, have it be a masseuse.

2. **Get psyched.** Before you leave, delve into the great books, movies, and *You Tube* videos that feature your destination. Start to follow local bloggers to get insider's tips. It will really enhance your experience to familiarize yourself with your chosen city's history, art, and cuisine. And though the natives you'll encounter will most likely speak English, learn at least some words of the beautiful language—*buon giorno, buona sera, grazie.* You'll be thrilled with the Italians' cheerful reaction to your efforts to speak even a little bit of their language.

3. **Spread the Word.** Tell your friends and family where you'll be traveling, and spread the word through your social media circles. Inevitably you'll find a connection—someone who has a friend or relative who lives in the place you're visiting, who you may be able to meet. Make contact in advance and enjoy time with a local. It'll be a treasured part of your trip.

4. **Go Solo.** Italy is a fantastic place to wander solo, following your very own desires. As Italians are such wonderfully social people, you'll rarely find yourself feeling lonely. Even when I'm traveling with my husband or girlfriends, I love having time on my own during the day to explore at my own pace— it makes dinner times more fun, when we join together to share our separate adventures. If you are on your own and would like to meet someone for dinner, there's an online resource, **Invite for a Bite** (www.inviteforabite.com), created for women travelers to connect while they're on the road. Or you could join a group tour that's focused on an active adventure, sightseeing, or a workshop that focuses on your interests. In other words, "I have no one to go with," doesn't have to be an obstacle to your Italian travel dreams.

5. **Flirting.** There's a shrink in New York who prescribes a trip to Italy for women who need a boost to their self-esteem. Italian men have mastered the art of flirting—it's one of the country's masterpieces. Females of all ages are adored here. Enjoy, without taking it too seriously. It's all in the spirit of: *You are women, we are men. We are alive! And what a fun game we play!* If you get harassment rather than flirting, a loud *"Vai Via"* ("Go Away") is the age-old stopper, and it usually works.

6. **Take a Guided Tour.** I resisted this for many trips, with visions of traipsing behind a screaming person hoisting an umbrella. At the same time I had the frustrating experiences of waiting in line for the Sistine Chapel while tour groups were ushered through in front of me, being baffled in the Forum where nothing is marked, and so on. It's great to join a *small* tour group—my favorite is Context Travel (www.contexttravel.com), a company that runs tours in Italy's major cities and limits them to six participants. Their guides are scholars and authors (not at all pretentious), so you get the experience of seeing a part of Italy with someone who's like an in-the-know friend. Check out my suggestions in the Online Resources section that follows.

7. **Stay Healthy.** You'll inevitably be in crowds of coughers, so starting with the airplane, take loads of Vitamin C and bring along anti-bacterial hand wash. And (God forbid), know that the number to dial for an ambulance is 118.

8. **Bidets** are found in almost every hotel room. Even in a simple convent where I stayed, there was a spigot gizmo attached to the toilet to serve the bidet purpose. Answers to most frequently asked questions: (1) you can sit either facing the faucet or not, (2) use after your normal toilet routine. To avoid surprises, test it out to see if it's the basin type or has squirting jets.

9. **Keep an Eye on Your Stuff.** Please don't become a paranoid traveler, but the truth is there are expert purse-snatchers out there, who target tourists in places of major distraction: public transportation, outdoor markets, and crowded

sights. Get your offensive style down, so it becomes second nature, and then you can roam around comfortably. While some prefer a secret money belt, neck pouch, or bra stuffing, I copy the native's style. Stand back and observe for a moment, and you'll catch on. I carry a shoulder bag tucked under my arm, always closed, on my inside-of-the-street arm, to avoid whizzing *motorini* thieves. At sidewalk restaurants, keep it hooked to you or your seat.

10. **Experience *Il Dolce Far Niente*—The Sweetness of Doing Nothing.** Though you'll have "must sees" on your itinerary, take time to escape from an agenda and simply be in the moment in Italy. It may be sleeping late with the sound of church bells in the distance, lingering at a caffè while beautiful-people-watching, or meandering around a garden—such bliss! Ideally, plan a "vacation from your vacation"—at least a day or two outside a city where *Il Dolce Far Niente* peacefully awaits.

Appendix 2
Budget Travel Tips

When to Go

November to Easter is Low Season (roughly), meaning that's when you'll find the lowest priced airfares and accommodations. This excludes Christmas week and *Carnevale* (around mid-February), in Venice.

Planning

* **Consider a Tour Package.** There are loads to choose from that offer low prices for airfare and hotels. Check out the offerings from the Italian Travel Promotional Council (www.goitpc.com), a group of experienced tour operators that collaborates with the Italian Government Tourist Board.

Airfare

* **Frequent Flyer Miles**: Great if you have them! Most of the time these have to be arranged far in advance, though you can get lucky last minute. It's often helpful to call the airline and speak to someone there who can let you know different ways of using them—such as flying in and out of different cities, alternate dates, and routes.

- **Flexibility is key to finding bargains**: Flying mid-week will save money, and you may consider flying into London, Paris, Amsterdam, or Frankfurt and then switching to a low cost European carrier, using www.whichbudget.com to search for the best deal.

- **Good websites to search for fares**: www.johnnyjet.com, www.kayak.com, www.airfarewatchdog.com, www.1800flyeurope.com

- **Sign up for airfare alerts**: You can put in your route (For example JFK-ROME) and you'll be notified when prices drop. Favorite websites: www.airfarewatchdog.com, www.kayak.com

- **Follow airlines on Twitter**: For up-to-the-minute notices on sales.

- **Use a travel agent**: It may seem old fashioned, and you will be charged a fee (about $25, average), but these pros are up on fare fluctuations and have access to inventories that can save you money.

Airport Transfers

Save on taxis to and from the airport, with these suitcase friendly options:

- **Rome**: Hop on the train, **Leonardo Express** (www.trenitalia.it, 14 euros), or a bus (www.terravision.eu or www.sitabusshuttle.com, about 4 euros). Though the bus is cheaper, it takes a little longer, and much longer if there's traffic. All run direct service between the airport to Rome's central train station, Termini, and you can take a cab from

there. Alternatively, a taxi costs a flat rate of 48 euros plus
1 euro per bag.

● **Florence**: Take the **Vola in Bus** (6 euros) from the airport
to Santa Maria Novella train station. Taxis charge 20 euros/
flat rate and 1 euro per bag.

● **Venice**: My favorite budget way is the **Alilaguna**
(www.alilaguna.it, 15 euros), a fast ferry that has a few different lines that can take you close to your destination. For
a little more, there is **Venice Link** (www.venicelink.com,
21 to 25 euros), a shared ferry, that offers discounts if you
buy online. A private ferry costs about 100 euros. There is
also a cheap bus (6 euros) that takes you from the airport
to the train station—but then you miss out on the fun way
of arriving in Venice via the water. **Bus info**: www.atvo.it,
www.actv.it.

Transportation

● **Discounts on train travel** are available if you plan ahead.
Just like airfares, tickets between the major cities (Rome-
Florence-Venice), usually get more expensive closer to
departure. A great new train service, **Italo Treno**
(www.italotreno.it), runs between the major cities, and
offers comfortable seating, free Wi-Fi, a cinema car, and
food by Eataly. Or there's the standard, **TrenItalia**
(www.trenitalia.it). Both websites offer special fares. For
regional travel (for example; from Florence to Prato),
TrenItalia is your only option and prices are low.

Accommodations

* **Best Hotel Discount Websites**: www.venere.com, www.booking.com, or the individual hotel website for promotional deals.

* **Hotel Alternatives**: You can get good prices if you consider staying in an **apartment** (many are available for three-day minimum stays), or a **B&B**. Many of the B&Bs have private bathrooms and there is great variation in size and style. There are also **convent or monastery stays**—just be aware that some have curfews. And finally **hostels**, many of which have changed over the years, offering rooms with private bathrooms, suites for families, as well as the traditional dorm-style accommodations.

* **For apartments and B&Bs for all cities**: www.AirBnB.com, www.bbitalia.it, www.bed-and-breakfast-in-italy.com

* **Convent or monastery stays**: www.monasterystays.com

* **Hostels**: www.hostelitaly.com

I've had wonderful experiences with these places:

* **Apartments and B&Bs In Rome**: www.romarentals.net, www.rentalinrome.com,

* **Apartment in Florence**: www.bepiolga.it

* **Apartment in Venice**: www.venicetostay.com

* **Favorite Rome convent stays**:
  Fraterna Domus, www.fraternadomus.it (also serves great lunches and dinners, but 11 p.m. curfew)
  Casa Santa Sofia, www.casasantasofia.it (no curfew, terrible food!)

- **Favorite Florence B&B**: For women only, www.forwomenonly-apartments.it
- **Favorite Venice budget choice**: Ca Centropietre, www.centopietre.net
- **Chic Venice Hostel**: www.generatorhostels.com, on Giudecca Island

Eating

You can eat well in Italy without spending a bundle. Do some restaurant research—check out the Online Resources suggestions here and suggestions in Golden Days. Avoid the obvious tourist spots near the major sights, and you'll be on the delicious track. Often one major sit-down meal a day will be satisfying, with lunch being the best choice for fancier eateries. House wine is generally good, and as far as tipping, ten percent is fine.

- **Budget options to consider for the evening** are **pizzerias** or **wine bars**, where you can fill up on delicious small plates of local specialties. With so many university students, Florence has many *Tavola Calda* (cafeteria-style places). Both Florence and Rome have a new tradition of *Aperitivi*, or **'Appy Hours**, where an antipasti buffet is spread out between 7 p.m. and 9 p.m. in a restaurant or bar, so for the price of a drink you can enjoy such goodies as *focaccia*, cheeses, and salumi.
- **Italian picnics are divine.** Buy cheeses, breads, olives, sweets, and wine at the local market, then enjoy lunch in a park or in the evening back in your hotel room, watching hilarious Italian TV.

Sightseeing

Rome, Florence, and Venice are open-air museums, where fountains, canals, and beautiful piazzas can all be enjoyed for free. Plus there are so many masterpieces of architecture and art inside the churches that don't cost a thing. For example in Rome there's the Pantheon and Saint Peter's Basilica with Michelangelo's Pieta, in Florence, The Duomo, and in Venice, San Marco.

Each city also offers combined ticket deals for sights and public transportation. Check out their websites and see if this will save you money, according to the time you have and your interests. You will also find info here regarding Free Museum days.

* **Rome:** www.romapass.it
* **Florence:** www.firenzecard.it, www.amicidegliuffizi.it, or check out www.florenceforfree.com
* **Venice:** www.veneziaunica.it

Souvenirs

Though it's worth it to spend money on the high quality artisan treasures each city offers, you can also pick up mementos that are not that expensive. It may sound corny, but I love having a towel from a Rome market with a Piazza Navona fountain on it in my Los Angeles kitchen, to bring back memories of my time there, and it's fun to bring something like that to friends back home as a hostess gift, wrapped around the neck of a wine bottle. Food is also always a good choice—from vacuum-packed cheeses, to chocolates, spices, or specialty sweets. The children in my life always appreciate Italian soccer shirts.

- **In Rome:** Aprons, kitchen gadgets, spices, and scarves from the markets, Vatican City mementos (such as rosary beads), soaps from the farmacia
- **Florence:** Scarves from the markets, artisan stationery, small leather items such as lipstick holders or eyeglass cases, soaps or scented candles from the farmacia
- **Venice:** Murano glass wine stoppers, mini Carnevale masks, artisan stationery

Appendix 3
Packing

What am I going to wear? This will undoubtedly be at the top of your thoughts once you book your trip.

Think simple: Italian women dress stylishly without a lot of fuss. Color coordinate, be neat, pack non-wrinkable fabrics, sunglasses, and all shall be well. Over packing will end up being a drag on your trip. You can always hand wash, or get to a laundry or dry cleaner while you're there. Plus, what's the hardship of *having* to buy extra clothes or shoes in Italy?

Tag your luggage: Include the phone number of your destination on a tag outside and inside, on the top layer of your packed suitcase, just in case your luggage gets misplaced.

Don't Pack

* **Your hairdryer:** Even budget hotels have them.
* **Spike heels:** They get stuck in the cobblestones.
* **Shorts:** You'll feel odd unless you're biking or on a beach.
* **Sneakers:** Meaning your gym shoes or white sneakers. That said, comfortable shoes are important, as you'll be doing lots of walking. Check out Ecco, Arches, or Aerosole for good styles. Rubber soles are best for hill towns, where leather slips on the slopes.

Do Pack

* **Umbrella**: To always carry with you on "iffy" weather days. You'll regret having to buy one from eager street vendors who jack up the price the moment the sky opens.

* **Tissues**: To double as toilet paper. There will inevitably be places that are lacking.

* **Band-Aids and moleskin**: In case of foot blisters.

* **Travel-sized toiletries**: This is the stuff that can really add weight, so bring only what you need, including sun block. Dry shampoo is a great invention for traveling—lightweight and time-saving. Hotels generally supply shampoo, conditioner, and body lotion. You don't want to be spending euros on this in Italy.

* **Bathing suit**: Even for non-beach vacations, so you're prepared for a spontaneous spa visit or a pool. *And* consider a bikini...*that's right!* Even if you feel like you're past bikini days, you'll see that Italian women of every shape and size wear them. Go ahead and join in on the pleasure.

* **Crossbody bag**: Make sure you have something comfortable to carry your essentials for those days of lots of walking.

* **Lightweight duffel bag**: To fill with souvenirs for your return trip.

* **Copy of your passport, credit card numbers, and toll-free numbers to call in case of credit card loss**: Give another copy and your itinerary to someone who can easily be reached, so they can be sent to you if necessary. Before you go, call your bank and credit card companies to give them a heads-up, as in these days of high security, they may block your card if they aren't forewarned about your foreign spending.

* **E-reader and smart phone:** Loaded up with the guides and apps about where you're going. If you must take a guide-book, rip out and pack only the pages that apply to your destination—don't take the whole heavy book.

* **Plug Adapter or Converter:** To use with your electronic devices, as Italy runs on a different electrical system than American.

* **Streetwise maps** for the cities you'll be visiting. These laminated, purse-friendly, well-indexed maps are far superior to the ones hotels and tourist kiosks hand out. And even if you're using GPS on your phone or tablet when you're on the go, they're great to have in your hotel room as you plan out your day. You can buy them in U.S. bookstores or online: www.streetwisemaps.com.

* *Italy: Instructions for Use* (www.italyinstructions.com): A unique, practical, lightweight guide and phrasebook containing all the nitty-gritty details you'll need as you travel—for trains, driving, eating, making phone calls, public transportation, etc.

Packing à la Susan

* **Use wire hangers:** I know Joan Crawford would be horrified, but putting all your clothes on wire hangers, which you then roll up in plastic to prevent wrinkling and then whoosh into your hotel closet when you arrive, cuts down on unpacking time, which gives you more time for Italy.

* **Have a dress rehearsal:** Here I go confessing my corny secret packing ritual: I take my inspiration from Cher in *Moonstruck*—the scene where she gets ready for her date with Nicholas Cage. To get psyched for my date with Italy, I put

my mirror center stage, have a glass of white wine nearby, Andrea Bocelli blaring in the background, and all the wardrobe possibilities on the bed, including jewelry and scarves. Then I dress for the plane, for that day I know I'll be touring a museum, for that special dinner, etc. Inevitably, this is where I'll figure out what to mix and match, what shoes won't work, and cut out half of what's on that bed. And so the light, lovely adventure begins...

Online Resources

GENERAL

* Italian Government Tourist Board, www.italia.it
* Italian Travel Promotional Council: www.goitpc.com, a group of expert tour operators

Up To Date Travel Advice

* Art Viva Italy Blog: blog.artviva.com
* Dream of Italy: www.dreamofitaly.com
* Go Italy: www.goitaly.about.com
* Italian Notebook: www.italiannotebook.com
* Italofile: www.italofile.com
* Italy Magazine: www.italymagazine.com
* My Melange: www.mymelange.com
* Slow Travel: www.slowtrav.com
* Walks of Italy: www.walksofitaly.com
* Wandering Italy: www.wanderingitaly.com

Tour Consultation and Travel Services

* Italian Concierge: www.italianconcierge.com

* Italy Beyond the Obvious: www.italybeyondtheobvious.com, + great travel posts
* La Dolce Via Travel: www.ladolceviatravel.com

And

* Becoming Italian Word by Word: www.becomingitalianwordbyword.typepad.com, for insights into Italian language and culture
* Life in Italy: www.lifeinitaly.com, for Italian culture
* Karen Brown's World of Travel: www.karenbrown.com, wonderful accommodation recommendations

Group or Private Walking Tours

* Context Travel: www.contexttravel.com
* Tours by Locals: www.toursbylocals.com
* Walks of Italy: www.walksofitaly.com

ROME
www.turismoroma.it

Private Guides

* Iris Carulli: www.imcarulli.com
* Reena Grewal: www.eyesofrome.com

Websites and Blogs

* Aglio, Olio e Peperoncino: www.agliooliopeperoncino.com
* Browsing Rome: www.browsingrome.com

- Elizabeth Minchilli in Rome: www.elizabethminchilliinrome
  .com
- Mozzarella Mamma: www.mozzarellamamma.com
- Parla Food: www.parlafood.com
- Revealed Rome: www.revealedrome.com
- Rick's Rome: www.rickzullo.com
- Rome Digest: www.romedigest.com
- Spotted by Locals: www.spottedbylocals.com/rome

FLORENCE
www.firenzeturismo.it

Private Guide
- Freya Middleton, www.freyasflorence.com

Websites and Blogs
- An American in Italy: www.anamericaninitaly.com
- At Home in Tuscany: www.athomeintuscany.org
- Art Trav: www.arttrav.com
- Florence for Free: www.florenceforfree.wordpress.com
- Girl in Florence: www.girlinflorence.com
- One Step Closer: www.onestepcloser.net
  (customized tourist itineraries)
- Over a Tuscan Stove: www.divinacucina.com (tops for
  restaurant recommendations)
- Tuscan Traveler: www.tuscantraveler.com

VENICE
www.turismovenezia.it

Private Guides

- Isabella Bariani: isa.bariani@alice.it
- Cristina Gregorin: www.slow-venice.com,
  www.blog.slow-venice.com

Websites and Blogs

- Allogi Barbaria Blog: www.alloggibarbaria.blogspot.com
- Contemporary Venice: www.contemporary-venice.com
- I Am Not Making This Up: www.iamnotmakingthisup.net
- Monica Cesarato: www.monicacesarato.com
- Venezia Blog: www.veneziablog.blogspot.com

Index

Acknowledgments

Grazie mille to all you *100 Places in Italy Every Woman Should Go* readers and travelers—especially you who wrote and showed up at events to tell me how the book inspired your Italian adventures. You've inspired me to keep sharing more of my own.

Always, I'm deeply grateful for the love and support of mia famiglia: dear husband Jonathon Leifer, my maternal Chirico/Spada line—here, in Italia, and in Paradiso, who started it all. Patti Sullivan, sister/editor, and the latest addition, stepgranddaughter Florence Cahn Norman, who makes my spirits soar.

Thanks to all the writers and bloggers who've inspired me, and to fabulous friends and colleagues for their smarts and for making life while writing and traveling in The Big Three more fun: Gioia Acon, Sheila Balter, Risa Bell, Anne Block, Liz Brewster, Iris Carulli, Rosanne Cofoid, Carol Coviello-Malzone, Sandy Cutrone, the D'Aquilas, Betsy deFries, Susan Engbrecht, Babs Fasano, Deb Gaughan, the Giulianos, Valentina Grossi Orzalesi, Inge Hansen, Heather Hanson, Karen Herbst, Jo Ann Locktov, Nan McElroy, Petulia Melideo, Joanne Morgante, Mario and Lexi Marmorestein, Kathy McCabe, Tom Paris, Veronica Puleo, Phil and Monica Rosenthal, Laura Sousounis, Kristin Stasiowski, Jessica Stewart, Monica Vidoni, and Louise Wright.

I'm grateful for the assistance of the Italian Government Tourist Board, including the wonderful Emanuela Boni in the Los Angeles office, and in New York Marzia Bortolin and Eugenio Magnani. Big thanks to publishers James O'Reilly and Larry Habegger at Travelers' Tales for our years of working together.

And grazie always to the people of Italy, whose astounding openness and generosity have made writing about this country a dream come true.

About the Author

Susan Van Allen is the author of *100 Places in Italy Every Woman Should Go* and *Letters from Italy: Confessions, Adventures, and Advice*. She has been traveling to Italy for more than thirty years and has written about her experiences for National Public Radio, *AFAR*, *Town & Country*, *Tastes of Italia*, and many other publications. She has also written for TV, on the staff of the Emmy Award-winning sitcom, *Everybody Loves Raymond*. When not traveling in Italy, she lives in Los Angeles with her husband. For more, go to www.susanvanallen.com.